- The more I read; the more I was convicted to become a better soul-winner.
  - Leslie – Wenatchee, Washington

- This is what American needs. Our Churches are falling apart and we need a national revival!
  - Laura – Goodyear, Arizona

- Send this book to every major pastor in America. We've got to do something before it is too late!
  - Richard – Vancouver, BC Canada

- I was shocked! I think all Christians should be. Where is the love for the lost we are supposed to feel? Guess we got ours, don't worry about anyone else. Wow, I faced with my own uncaring attitude and this book woke me up. I truly don't want anyone to go to hell and I have to do my part as commanded by Christ and witness to the lost.
  - Greg – Riverside, California

This book is designed to shake up the Christian world. There are untold millions dying without Christ and going to hell for eternity. We are failing as Christian Churches and as Christians. We are failing our children and our nation. We badly need a wake-up call and this book provides it.

Floyd C. McElveen

The Late Great American Church

Is the Sun Setting on the American Church?

Floyd C. McElveen

Big Mac Publishers   Riverside, Ca 92504

The Late Great American Church

Copyright © 2009 by Floyd C. McElveen
All rights reserved. Permission is granted to copy or reprint portions for any noncommercial use, except they may not be posted online without permission.

Author: Floyd C. McElveen
Editor: Greg Bilbo
Proofreader Leslie Williamson
Cover photo © 2009: IStockPhoto.com
Cover Illustration / Design: Greg Bilbo

Unless otherwise indicated, Scripture quotations are from:
The Holy Bible, New King James Version © 1984 by Thomas Nelson, Inc.
Other Scripture quotations are from:
The Holy Bible, New International Version (NIV) © 1973, 1984, 1995, 2002 by International Bible Society, used by permission of Zondervan Publishing House
New American Standard Bible (NASB) © 1960, 1977, Lockman Foundation
The Holy Bible, King James Version (KJV)

Library of Congress Control Number: 2009933505
Library of Congress subject headings:
1. REL030000   RELIGION / Christian Ministry / Evangelism
2. REL045000   RELIGION / Christian Ministry / Missions
3. REL080000   RELIGION / Christian Ministry / Preaching

BIASC / BASIC Classification Suggestions:
1. Evangelism (Christian theology)
2. Evangelism for laymen.
3. Evangelism -- United States -- Controversial literature.

ISBN-13: 978-0-9823554-5-9
ISBN-10: 0-9823554-5-9
1.0

Published by Big Mac Publishers
www.bigmacpublishers.com / Riverside, California 92504
Printed and bound in the United States of America

Table of Contents

DEDICATION	IV
PREFACE	V
INTRODUCTION	XI
THE "MANGLED BODIES" HOLOCAUST	1
MURDER IN THE CHURCH?	13
BLOODY HANDS, BROKEN HEARTS AND LOST SOULS	49
WHAT DOES THE HOLY SPIRIT USE TO BRING MEN TO CHRIST?	63
THE TRUE STATE OF THE UNSAVED	79
THE CHRISTIAN HOLOCAUST	99
GOODBYE "CHRISTIAN" AMERICA: THE DESPERATE NEED OF DYING CHURCHES	113
NATIONAL PRAYER	134
OTHER BOOKS BY FLOYD C. MCELVEEN	137

Dedication

I dedicate this book to my dear friend and long time supporter, Richard Hughes. He supplied all the financing and offered many valuable suggestions. He has a heart for the lost and uses his resources to reach souls for Christ. I deeply appreciate all he has done.

Floyd C. McElveen

Preface

One area of clarification I want to discuss is the proper distinction between the roles of America, the Church, and Christians. Two friends of mine, each a strong theologian, have divergent views on this subject.

One believes we should enter politics and fight against every attempt to sequester, destroy, or invalidate Christianity. We should object en masse to every encroachment by government via activist judges, corrupt government, and removal of the Ten Commandments from public buildings, along with laws that inhibit Christianity and violate our rights, calling evil good and good evil, etc.

The other believes that repentance and prayer, consistently and fervently calling on a Sovereign God to act in our behalf, informing our people what is going on, praying for revival, and living a pure and holy life ourselves, while demanding the same of our representatives, is the way to go.

I see virtue in both views. We must arise and take our government back, or America is doomed, but we must do it in Christian love and by peaceful means. Many of our religious and political leaders today seem cowardly, paralyzed by fear, or this reprehensible deterioration could never have occurred.

My problem is that America is largely defined by Christianity, and Christianity is so entwined in government it is difficult to separate the two. Though this is not a theocracy, as Israel was, it was once the most Christian nation on earth, with the intent of permanently affecting our government and all of our lives. For a while, it did, but that day is fast passing away. More missionaries were sent out from America to reach millions for Christ than anywhere else in the world.

Patriotism to a corrupt nation, instead of to Christ, is not necessarily a virtue. Moreover, we are rapidly becoming a corrupt nation, endorsing, in some cases, homosexual marriages, abortions (even cruel and barbaric partial birth abortions), fraud, criminal activity, and immorality that would have made earlier generations blanch. Today, what affects America affects the church, and what affects the church affects America, whether the secular progressives want to acknowledge it or not. It should not be so; the church should make a tremendous impact on America, by its holiness, evangelistic zeal, and opposition to evil. America should not adversely impact the church by the government, corrupt society, or cultural miasma. But it does!

May God help us get back to our moorings for His sake, the sake of our children, and the last hope of a vanishing America we once knew, loved, and fought for.

Yes, America was a Christian Nation, founded as such—

not by any means claiming that all its citizens were Christians—but this is the foundation of America.

If you have a desire to read further on this issue, please, at any cost, get David Barton's book, *The Myth of Separation*, Wallbuilders Press, P.O. Box 397, Aledo, Texas 76008, or phone (817) 441-6044. He also has other later books available.

I spoke on this subject in a previous book, asserting that, "*In the Mayflower Compact* it was clearly stated that spreading the Gospel of the Lord Jesus Christ, as well as freedom to worship without being under a mandated State church, was their purpose" (*The Faith of An Atheist, 2009, p. 63).*

Furthermore, Patrick Henry endorsed and accentuated this, when he wrote in 1776, "It cannot be emphasized too strongly or too often that this great nation was founded not by religionists, but by Christians, not on religion, but on the Gospel of Jesus Christ. For that reason alone people of other faiths have been afforded freedom of worship here."

Incredibly, 52 of the 55 signers of the Declaration of Independence were orthodox, deeply committed Christians.

Pay attention to this quote from David Barton's book, in which he is speaking of the source of our Constitution:

What was that source? The Bible! The Bible accounted for 34% of all the founders quotes. Another 60% of their quotes were drawn from authors who had derived their ideas from the Bible. Therefore it can be shown that 94% of their quotes are based either directly or indirectly on the Bible. Even major news magazines have conceded that "historians are discovering that the Bible, perhaps even more than the Constitution is our Founding document" (*The Myth of Separation, 1992, p. 201).*

Finally, consider the following article written by Moody Adams on 6/23/2009, in *MoodyNews*:

WHY CHRISTIANITY IS NOT WORKING

The church no longer sets the moral standards for America. Her baptisms, attendance and finances are on the decline. Her pastors have a divorce record as bad as the general public. Her youth's conduct is little better than that of the pagans.

These problems are all the result of one failing: the church is only carrying out half the great commission. Jesus not only said to "Go ye into all the world, and preach the gospel to every creature" (Mark 16:15). He also commissioned the church to "Teaching them to observe all things whatsoever I have commanded you" (Matthew 28:20).

We have been carrying out one-half of the Great Commission, preaching the gospel, but not teaching them to obey His commands.

Some have completely ignored Christ's commands; saying believing on the Lord Jesus Christ is all we need to save us that that is all we want.
Others scream, "Legalism" and "*Works* Salvation" if you mention a need for obedience.

Preface

Obedience is not a condition of salvation, but a result of salvation. Obeying my wife's commands was not a condition of being married. I try to please her because I am married, I love her, and I delight in pleasing her.

Henry T. Blackaby, Southern Baptist's spokesman on "Experiencing God" writes, "If Southern Baptists want to see a 'Great Commission Resurgence,' they need to focus on the relationship between disciples and the living Lord Jesus, not just launch a new emphasis on evangelism.

"I have felt for a long time that Southern Baptist have focused on evangelism and missed discipleship," Blackaby told the Baptist Press on May 11, 2009.

"The most important part of the Great Commission is to teach them to practice everything I have commanded you.' That's discipleship and that's the heart of the Great Commission."

Without commands and obedience we are little more than animals. "By obedience we are made a society and a republic, and distinguished from herds of beasts, and heaps of flies, who do what they list and are incapable of laws," said Jeremy Taylor.

The godly A.W. Tozer aptly said, "Have you noticed how much praying for revival has been going on of late - and how little revival has resulted? I believe the problem is that we have been trying to substitute praying for obeying, and it simply will not work. To pray for revival while ignoring the plain precept laid down in Scripture is to waste a lot of words and get nothing for our trouble. Prayer will become effective when we stop using it as a substitute for obedience."

The Commandments of Christ are the key to turning America back to God, transforming our families and business.

Study His commands, meditate on them, teach them and above all else, obey them.   (End of Article)

Yes, we *were* a Christian Nation, and there may still be hope, but it is fading fast. Do something if you are a true Christian; take a stand, as God leads you. Pray. Join with others to stop this devilish erosion of our freedoms by our government, and sometimes even our flaccid churches.

Introduction

A few years ago, I wrote a book titled *Unashamed, A Burning Passion to Share The Gospel*. It was a heartfelt plea to get Christians to become soul-winners. As a missionary to Alaska, church planter, evangelist, soul-winner, pastor, and author, I was very heavy-hearted over the few Christians, about two or three percent, who ever lead anyone to Christ. Ninety-seven to ninety-eight percent never do. I believed then, as I do now, that this is the major reason millions worldwide go to Hell without a Savior. Some never even share their faith; much less win anyone to Christ.

The *Unashamed* book, renamed *So Send I You* and now being re-published by Big Mac Publishers, was highly endorsed by Dr. Jerry Falwell, Dr. John Ankerberg, Dr. John Morris, Dr. Marshall Maculuso and Dr. Herbert Anderson (although we did not get his glowing testimonial in print). Dr. Robert Sumner gave it a sparkling review in his great magazine, *The Biblical Evangelist*.

The book was carefully written, answering the myriad excuses I have run against in evangelistic meetings; seeking Scripture and the Holy Spirit to arouse the soul-winning fire in my beloved America. I was not at all satisfied with the results, so we are re-publishing the book under the title of *So Send I You*, my first choice, really. I pray God will use it.

This book in your hands however, unleashes what I believe to be God's true heartbreak, and mine, over lost souls. It is meant as Shock Therapy.

In powerful meetings on the Kenai Peninsula in Alaska, God raised up on-fire soul-winners, some of whom became preachers of the Gospel, when I preached on "Are you soul-winners, or soul-murderers?" Heavy conviction followed initial anger, and tears and revival resulted (not just from this message, but it was part of the mix).

In that sermon, I used the following passage from Ezekiel as a basis for my plea:

"When I say unto the wicked, O wicked man, thou shalt surely die; if thou dost not speak to warn the wicked from his way, that wicked man shall die in his iniquity; but his blood will I require at thine hand" (Ezekiel 33:8).

This may be speaking of the watchman who did not warn those physically and/or possibly spiritually headed for death. God could have sovereignly saved the people, but He did not. He depended on the watchman to warn them. If he did not, the wicked died, unwarned, and their blood was on the watchman's hands. How much more awful not to warn those God has commissioned us to warn who are headed for eternal Hell? It may not be said *literally* that professing Christians have blood on their hands, as the New Testament does not affirm this, but it does illustrate vividly the guilt of those who do not witness.

Introduction

Just because I was very successful using that approach in preaching, does not mean (1) that it was necessarily right or (2) that it would have the same impact in writing as it did in preaching. I personally believe that Ezekiel 33:8 speaks of the possible execution of the unfaithful watchmen, who did not warn the wicked. Blood on the hands has strong connotations of a murder committed.

Yet I assumed, and still do, that anyone in a church congregation understood immediately that there was no literal blood on their hands. Like many strong illustrations from the Old Testament, I believed they would identify with the watchman if they themselves were not speaking to warn the wicked, and realize that it was a very serious matter with God. The "blood on the hands" illustration might break otherwise hardened hearts.

In addition, I wanted them, by the Holy Spirit, to check their own hearts. How, dear God, how, could someone with Jesus and His incontrovertible passion for the lost, and His burning love to save them, not care enough to at least witness? Where is the love of Jesus in such a life? I wanted them to examine their hearts by the Word of God and by the Holy Spirit to find if they really were saved. Certainly, a continual life of such self-centered abandonment of the lost for whom Christ died is a very bad omen.

Not knowing their hearts, I certainly cannot make a judgment, but I strongly suspect that such have never tasted the sweet wine of His love, reveled in His awesome power, rejoiced in His forgiveness, and had His love for the lost implanted in their hearts.

Please read this book, asking God to break your heart for souls, as His is broken. I believe many of you will be transformed forever. And become soul-winners. And please get the book, *So Send I You*. These two books go together.

(One vital thing you can do is to get this book in bulk from the publisher, and spread it around in your community, your churches, friends and relatives, and leaders you know. We will make it as cheap as possible.)

The "Mangled Bodies" Holocaust

For the preaching of the cross is to them that perish foolishness; but unto us which are saved it is the power of God (I Corinthians 1:18).

As a missionary to Alaska, church planter, and pastor, I can offer valuable insights from my own studies and experiences. For 10 years, I acted as National Evangelist of Mission Doors, formerly The Conservative Baptist Home Mission Society, and Mission to the Americas. Even more specifically, I speak from personal experience as a long-time evangelist, personal soul-winner, and author.

Could it be that as much as 90 percent of today's "Christians," are false converts doomed to hell? God forbid, yet consider the evidence.

Some of the following material on the following page, I have gathered from Ray Comfort and his powerful book, *Revivals Golden Key*, now renamed *The Way of the Master*. Various statistics come from Josh McDowell's advertising material and from pollster George Barna's surveys and polls.

The sad condition of "Christians" and the church:

1. Report on a 1990 U.S.A. Crusade. 600 decisions. Follow-up 90 days later. Not even one continued in his or her faith. Backsliders? No! False converts.

2. Cleveland, Ohio. Inner City Campaign. 400 decisions for Christ. Not even one followed through with their decision.

3. 1985 four day Crusade. 217 decisions. 92 percent fell away.

4. Charles E. Hackett, National Home Missions Director for the Assemblies of God in the U.S. said that about 95 out of 100 of those who make decisions at the altar will not become integrated into the church. "In fact most of them will not return for a second visit," said Hackett.

5. Ernest C. Reisinger, in his book, *Today's Evangelism*, said of an eight-day outreach, that there were 68 "conversions." He added that a month later not one of the "converts" could be found.

6. In 1991, organizers of a Salt Lake City outreach encouraged follow-up. They said that less than five percent of those who made decisions during a crusade were living a Christian life one year later. In other words, 95 percent were false converts.

7. A Boulder, Colorado pastor sent a team to Russia in 1991 and reported 2,500 decisions. The next year they found only 30 going on in their faith. Only a little more than one percent proved true to Christ.

Chapter One – The Mangled Bodies Holocaust

8. In Leeds, England, a U.S. speaker got 400 decisions for a local church. Six weeks later only two were going on, and they eventually fell away.

9. In November 1970, many churches combined for an evangelistic outreach in Ft. Worth, Texas. There were 30,000 decisions. Six months later the follow-up committee could find only 30 going on in their faith. One out of a thousand; about one-tenth of one percent!

10. A mass crusade by America's greatest evangelist reported 18,000 decisions. 94 percent failed to be incorporated into a local church.

11. In Sacramento, California, a combined crusade brought in 2,000 "decisions for Christ." One church followed up 52 of those decisions and could not find one conversion.

12. A leading U.S. denomination reported that in 1995 they had 384,057 decisions. Only 22,983 were retained in church fellowships. They could not account for 361,074 supposed conversions! That is a 94 percent fall-away rate. (Even so, this tragic loss is one of the "better" results.)

13. In Omaha, Nebraska, the pastor of a large church said he was involved in a crusade where 1,300 decisions were made, and not even one "convert" continued on in his or her faith.

14. Pastor Dennis Grenell from Auckland, New Zealand, has traveled to India every year since 1980. He reported that he saw 80,000 decision cards stacked in a hut in the city of Rajamundry, the "results" of past evangelistic crusades. Nev-

3

ertheless, he claimed that one would be fortunate to find even 80 Christians in the entire city.

15. In the *American Horizon*, March/April issue, 1993, the National Director of Home Missions for a major U.S. denomination disclosed the fact that in 1991, 11,500 churches had obtained 294,784 decisions for Christ. Unfortunately, they could find only 14,337 in fellowship. That means that (no doubt despite the usual intense follow-up) they could not account for approximately 280,000 of those who made decisions.

16. A major Christian TV network interviewed a Russian Christian leader on July 5, 1996. She said of Russian converts, "Many thousands have received salvation and healing...but because of there not being many leaders, not many stayed with their faith." True, follow-up (discipleship) is essential and biblical, but whatever happened to God's promise in Jude 24, "Now unto him that is able to keep you from falling, and to present you faultless before the presence of His glory with exceeding joy..." Who discipled the Ethiopian eunuch?

17. Churches in America are closing at a rate of 3,500 to sometimes 6,000 a year. One of the major Evangelical denominations in the United States, with approximately 30,000 churches, in a recent year had 10,000 churches that did not report *one baptism!* Whatever are they doing? The *Baptist Record of Mississippi* several months ago reported that, according to a nationwide survey, 88 percent of our young people at age 18 leave the church and never come back! Billy

Chapter One – The Mangled Bodies Holocaust

Graham said that he believed that 70 percent of our church members were unsaved. Some have estimated as high as 90 percent of our "Christians" are not Christians at all. They have made a profession of faith in Christ and continue to go their own way, be their own gods, and run their own lives, with some religious activity thrown in—when it is convenient.

•

For the most part, modern Christianity is either quiescent, or actively involved in, immorality, fornication, adultery, perversion, covetousness (which is idolatry, which is eternally fatal), self-centeredness, and following a false culture hostile to Christianity. There are other more subtle departures from God in pride, arrogance, envy, jealousy, anger, and relying on science, psychology, or peer groups rather than God's word, the Bible. This can lead to dropping out, or attending church perfunctorily. Often this is followed by seeking Biblically forbidden pleasures, and trying to live for God on the one hand, and self and the world on the other.

Most of our college-bound young people lose their faith before they graduate. If you think a mind is a terrible thing to waste—what about a soul?

This does not catch God by surprise! He predicted that there would be a great falling away in the last days, with apostasy being rampant. Hear, and indeed feel, the pathos in the question of the Lord Jesus Christ in Luke 18:8b, ". . .

Nevertheless, when the Son of man cometh, shall he find faith on the earth?"

Indeed, listen to some of the things that God's Word says will characterize the last days, and some of the professing Christians of the last days.

They profess that they know God; but in works they deny him, being abominable, and disobedient, and unto every good work reprobate (Titus 1:16).

This know also, that in the last days perilous times shall come. For men shall be lovers of their own selves, covetous, boasters, proud, blasphemers, disobedient to parents, unthankful, unholy, Without natural affection, trucebreakers, false accusers, incontinent, fierce, despisers of those that are good, Traitors, heady, high-minded, lovers of pleasures more than lovers of God; Having a form of godliness, but denying the power thereof: from such turn away (II Timothy 3:1-5).

Many of those described above are obviously professing Christians, but almost certainly are not true Christians.

More Devastating Facts!

Josh McDowell, probably relying in part on the statistics of professional pollster George Barna, claims that:

Chapter One – The Mangled Bodies Holocaust

- 63 percent of our church youth do not believe that Jesus is the son of the true God.
- 58 percent believe that various faiths teach the same truths.
- 68 percent do not believe the Holy Spirit is a real entity (person).
- 70 percent do not believe absolute moral truth exists.

"Why do beliefs matter?" asks McDowell.
"Why does truth matter?" asks McElveen

Why? Because people with these false beliefs and concepts are:
- 200 percent more likely to physically harm someone.
- 216 percent more likely to be resentful.
- 300 percent more likely to use illegal drugs.
- 600 percent more likely to commit suicide.

Most terrible of all, without repentance and true faith in the Lord Jesus Christ, 100 percent of these are sure of going to an everlasting Hell!

When we talk of soul-winning, we are talking of leading people by the power of the Holy Spirit, to a heart committal to Jesus Christ, based on His death, shed blood on the cross for us, and His burial and resurrection.

We are talking of a 100 percent know-so salvation that changes one's life here and now. (See I John 5:13 and II Corinthians 5:17.) We are talking of the certainty of going to Heaven, and not to Hell. We are talking of a salvation decision that leads to a deep love for Jesus Christ. This decision will lead to sweet fellowship with Him, and joyful obedience.

Consider I Corinthians 16:22 carefully, prayerfully. "If any man love not the Lord Jesus Christ, let him be Anathema, Maranatha." (According to *Vines Expository Dictionary*, Maranatha, sometimes, was an exclamation, meaning simply, "Oh Lord, come.") Maranatha deals with the coming of Jesus Christ for His own. Anathema deals with being accursed or cut off from Christ, forever. This is declared to be the fate of all those who say they believe the facts about Jesus Christ, His death, burial and resurrection, declare they have made a decision for salvation, yet adamantly refuse to live for Jesus, and continue going their own way, living for the world, the flesh, and the devil.

A belief in Jesus Christ, which does not lead to a real heart love for Him, is fatal folly and dooms irretrievably to Hell.

God tells us what identifies love. "Jesus answered and said, 'If a man love me, he will keep my words: and my Father will love him, and we will come unto him, and make our abode with him'" (John 14:23). "He that loveth me not keepeth not my sayings..." (v. 24). A person can outwardly obey Christ and not love Him, which is legalism, but a person who truly loves Christ will obey Him.

I believe in eternal security for those who truly believe in Christ (see John 3:36a, and a host of other verses), but today

Chapter One – The Mangled Bodies Holocaust

that teaching is being used to cover the sins and rebellion of perhaps millions of professing Christians. So is false teaching about the wonderful grace of God, which is often distorted to cover antinomianism, and lasciviousness. I have quoted God's definition of grace in this book, *but it is so important…here it is again!*

For the grace of God that bringeth salvation hath appeared to all men, Teaching us that, denying ungodliness and worldly lusts, we should live soberly, righteously, and godly, in this present world; Looking for that blessed hope, and the glorious appearing of the great God, and our Saviour Jesus Christ; Who gave himself for us, that he might redeem us from all iniquity, and purify unto himself a peculiar people, zealous of good works (Titus 2:11-14).

My heart aches when I think of those trusting in the false security of a belief that does not save, a life that is not changed, a grace on which they presume, and a Christ they do not love enough to repent of their sins and follow Him with their whole heart. I was once one of those, until He opened my eyes and saved me. Thank God for His true grace and love! Only Christ can thus change a life, but we must present Him with compassion and love, and Biblical clarity as to what real salvation in Christ is all about.

When a person is truly saved, now, in this life, there is a new sweetness, a new joy, victory over sins, help with problems, joy, and fellowship with Jesus and other believers, deep worship and appreciation of Jesus. Paul could rejoice, even in dank, dark prisons, and told us to rejoice always (Philippians 4:4). True Christians know the answer to life, where we came from, why we are here, and where we are going when we die. We have a new and passionate purpose.

As far as I know, our life here on earth is the only time forever we can prove our love for Jesus Christ, in suffering, in fighting the world, the flesh and the devil, in faithfulness to Him, His church, and His Word. It is the only time we can win lost souls to Him, the most wonderful privilege ever granted to man, the elixir of the Christian life.

Yet the most important thing of all is that we will be in Heaven with Jesus, with no sin, pain, separation, or suffering forever. We have escaped the Lake of Fire, the horrible suffering of the lost, where those who enter abandon all hope. Hell is forever. Forever. Think about it.

Nevertheless, when we enter most Christian bookstores, we find hundreds of books on how to solve problems, conquer bad habits, enjoy life more, get along with obnoxious people, love one another, etc. We find few, if any, books on judgment, Heaven or Hell, and maybe a few on witnessing but not offending people.

The main concentration of book topics, along with the culture and the acquiescence of many pastors and Bible teachers, seems to be on the here and now. The here and now, and our walk with Jesus now, is vitally important, but was never meant to obfuscate the main purpose Jesus died for, not just for the here and now, although that is included.

Chapter One – The Mangled Bodies Holocaust

The here and now is just a flash in the infinity of time. Heaven and Hell are forever. There are only two places to go when you die, either Heaven or Hell. Jesus died for you and me, and shed His precious blood for us, so that we could go to Heaven with Him forever, and not to Hell.

The Late Great American Church

Chapter Two – Murder in the Church?

Murder in the Church?

When I say unto the wicked, O wicked man, thou shalt surely die; if thou dost not speak to warn the wicked from his way, he shall die in his iniquity; but his blood will I require at your hands (Ezekiel 33:8).

Silent Christians are a disgrace to God, and a juxtaposition of everything he taught!

Let the redeemed of the Lord say so, whom he hath redeemed from the hand of the enemy (Psalm 107:2).

Also I say unto you, "Whosoever shall confess me before men, him shall the Son of man also confess before the angels of God: But he that denieth me before men shall be denied before the angels of God" (Luke 12:8-9).

That if thou shalt confess with thy mouth the Lord Jesus, and shalt believe in thine heart that God hath raised him from the dead, thou shalt be saved. For with the heart man believeth unto righteousness; and with the mouth confession is made unto salvation (Romans 10:9-10).

David, in agony of soul, confessed his sin with Bathsheba, and his brokenness and shame, after admitting his sin in deep contrition, in Psalm 51:1-11. He asked for forgiveness, cleansing, restoration, a clean heart, and a right spirit. He then adds, "Restore unto me the joy of my salvation; and uphold me with thy free spirit, then will I teach transgressors thy ways; and sinners shall be converted to thee" (v. 12-13).

Forgiven sinners, or forgiven saints, will teach transgressors about the Lord Jesus Christ, and sinners will get saved! (Incidentally, I have heard professing Christians who were living in sin erroneously use David as an example). You cannot read New Testament grace in the Church age back into the lives of Old Testament Saints! David was a precious saint of God, a man after God's own heart, but the standard is much higher now. We have the light of Jesus now. We have the full and complete Word of God; they did not.

The Old Covenant (Old Testament) and the Ten Commandments, blood sacrifices, and ceremonial laws revealed God's Holiness, and condemned man's sinfulness. Man could not be saved by his own efforts, and stood guilty before a Holy God. Grace was extended as man's sins were covered by blood sacrifices, pointing to the one who would make one sacrifice forever for our sins. The New Covenant, (New Testament) puts man in a whole new relationship to God, because now his sins are not just covered, but taken away by the Lord Jesus Christ, who was hailed by John the Baptist, as he said, "...Behold the Lamb of God, which taketh away the sin of the world" (John 1:29b).

Thus, God exults in Hebrews, "But now hath he obtained a more excellent ministry, by how much also he is the mediator of a better covenant, which was established upon better

Chapter Two - Murder In The Church

promises. For if that first covenant had been faultless, then should no place have been sought for a second" (8:6-7).

We have the Holy Spirit dwelling permanently within us; they did not. "I will pray the Father, and he shall give you another Comforter, that he may abide with you forever; Even the Spirit of truth; whom the world cannot receive, because it seeth him not, neither knoweth him: but ye know him; for he dwelleth *with* you, and shall be *in* you" (John 14:16-17, emphasis added).

We have had the Lord Jesus Christ, God in the flesh, come and spend years on earth teaching the disciples, and through them, us. They did not. We have Jesus living in us and living His life through us, on a permanent basis. They did not. We have had many more prophecies fulfilled, to cement our faith; we have had the Prophesied One, the Messiah, come and dwell among us, and fulfill hundreds of prophecies. They did not. We have realized the fulfillment of the promise of the cross. They did not. We have the glorious resurrection of the Lord Jesus Christ. They did not. We have the Church, and its officers, its fellowship, its ordinances, its functions, its gifts shaping the body of Christ, and the incredible access to technology, printing, media and world outreach. They did not.

They had grace, for only by grace can anyone be saved, but now we live in the very age of grace. We are looking daily for His soon return, and that too has a purifying effect on His people (see I John 3:2-3). Under grace and God's standard for the Church age, David could not even have been a deacon in the local church! A deacon has to be the husband of one wife.

Look at the cost of David's deadly dalliance with the beautiful, voluptuous, Bathsheba. David committed adultery, then perjury, and the proxy murder of a good man, Uriah, Bathsheba's husband.

Then, agony unspeakable! Broken fellowship with the God David loved. The death of his precious little baby, born of his lustful relationship with Bathsheba. The rape of his virgin daughter, Tamar, by her brother, Amnon. The murder of Amnon by vengeful Absalom, another of David's sons. The years without Absalom after he fled. (Even after his return, David seemed somewhat estranged from his son.) The rebellion of Absalom and many of David's people, as Absalom sought to be King, and lured many to rebel with him. The open polluting of the land by Absalom's going in to David's concubines (servant wives). David fleeing for his life and the tremendous battle in the forest of Ephraim, where 20,000 people died! Absalom, once the apple of David's eye, killed in ignominy.

Imagine David, with inconsolable grief over the death of his son, Absalom. Hear his heart cry as he learns of the death of his beloved son in battle, "And the king was much moved, and went up to the chamber over the gate, and wept: and as he went, thus he said, 0 my son, Absalom, my son, my son Absalom! Would God I had died for thee, 0 Absalom, my son, my son!" (II Samuel 18:33).

Chapter Two - Murder In The Church

What a price for adultery. Yet in the New Testament it seems worse. "Know ye not that the unrighteous shall not inherit the kingdom of God?" (I Corinthians 6:9). Then follows a list of the unrighteous, and included among those who shall not inherit the kingdom of God, are adulterers.

Later, after David got old, he had a beautiful girl to marry and minister to him, named Abishag, but he had no sexual relationship with her as a wife. David anointed Solomon, his son by Bathsheba, to be King, as he had promised. Yet Adonijah, David's son by Haggith, tried to usurp the Kingship and the Kingdom. Solomon spared Adonijah death, but later, Adonijah asked to be given Abishag for his wife.

Sensing plot and rebellion, Solomon, put his own brother (or half-brother) to death, and then had Joab, mighty leader of David's army (who had been faithful to David for many years), put to death! Joab had followed Adonijah in his rebellion. Even for a believer, the price of fornication and adultery is formidable, with consequences horrendous, for oneself and for ones loved ones! That was in the Old Testament. The standard under grace in the New Testament is even higher. Jesus taught that to look on a woman and lust after her is adultery; He also taught that adulterers do not inherit the kingdom of God (see I Corinthians 6: 9-11).

Adulterers go to Hell, unless they are forgiven by the blood of the Lord Jesus Christ and repent and get delivered from their adulterous lifestyle—past, present, and future. I have drawn this out, because when we talk about soul-winning we are not talking just about a decision, even though that is indispensable to salvation, but a changed life resulting from that decision, which invites Christ to rule in one's life as Lord and Savior.

That brings us to pornography, which is saturating American society today. I understand it is in the life of many "Christians," and sometimes, even preachers. It is not harmless; it is hellish. God loves you and Jesus will deliver you, because He came to save His people *from* their sins. Pornography is another gateway to Hell! Quit it! Flee it!

We made this parenthetical detour for a reason. Note Proverbs 24:

If thou forbear to deliver them that are drawn unto death, and those that are ready to be slain; If thou sayeth, Behold, we knew it not; doth not he that pondereth the heart consider it? And he that keepeth thy soul, doth not he know it? And shall not he render to every man according to his works? (Proverbs 24: 11-12.)

Inevitably, there is a penalty for those who have the means of deliverance for those threatened by physical death, or those threatened by spiritual death, if they fail to deliver them, and yet make excuses!

We have considered the result of David's horrible sin. What about yours and mine?

We are told that only about two or three percent of Christians ever lead anyone to Christ, and many, even of those, do so very inconsistently! Yet in Ezekiel we read that if we do

Chapter Two – Murder In The Church

not speak to warn the wicked, we have blood on our hands. That speaks of murder! The murder of lost souls by neglect. It speaks of adultery. Loving the world more than we love Jesus, which God assures us is spiritual adultery, which is even more deadly than physical adultery! Today, the Church may have blood on its hands. Christians may have blood on their hands. If so, are we not guilty of the murder of millions of lost souls?

Some very sharp Bible students tell me that God would never let anyone go to Hell because of someone else's sin. No, of course not. People go to Hell because of their own sin. However, men might not be going to Hell if Adam had not sinned, so to some extent, we do go to Hell in part because of someone else's sin, plus our own!

Both as a missionary and as an evangelist, I believed that many go to Hell who would have turned from their sins to Jesus if someone had given them the Gospel. I still do. That is why I went through the sacrifices, hardship, and freezing cold, putting my family at risk in the old days in wild Alaska.

Some people believe that if you do not go out and share the Gospel you may merely miss a blessing or lose a reward; that God will raise up someone in your place to go to those who otherwise would not hear. Therefore, no one will ever go to Hell simply because he or she has not heard the Gospel.

According to this view, New Testament Christians certainly do not have blood on their hands, as Ezekiel 33:8 declares, because this passage was referring to a watchman designated to watch over and guard the children of Israel against an enemy. Not all the Israelites were thus designated, not even the godly ones, as far as we know. A trumpet of alarm was to be blown, and all were to take heed, or bear their own folly, if they did not.

It seems that in conjunction with this warning, the narrative swings to Ezekiel as the "son of man," who is declared a watchman, particularly to warn the "wicked." Though the wicked man (or men) fails to repent, the watchman has "delivered his *own* soul," a very pungent statement, (emphasis added). If the watchman did not speak to warn the wicked, the wicked man died in his iniquity. (Note that God did NOT send *someone else* to warn him, a popular fallacy.) Then God declared with ominous admonition, ". . . his blood will I require at thine hands," speaking of the hands of the unfaithful watchman, who let a wicked man die in his sins without warning him.

While this is only one of many soul-winning messages I have given, and thousands have responded, this is one of the most powerful.

Jesus Himself led the way in soul-winning with His witness to Nicodemus, in John 3, and to the woman at the well in John 4. He sent His disciples out two by two, to witness, preach, evangelize, or whatever term includes sharing Christ and winning souls.

Thus, He reinforced the warning in Ezekiel, and the same theme in Proverbs 24:11-12, with urgency. "If thou forbear to deliver them that are drawn unto death, and those that are ready to be slain; If thou sayest, Behold, we knew it not; doth

Chapter Two – Murder In The Church

not he that pondereth the heart consider it? And he that keepeth thy soul, doth not he know it? And shall not he render to every man according to his works?"

If we have the means, we are responsible to deliver those who are about to be slain. This may be speaking of physical death, but no matter. How much more egregious, infinitely more terrible, if men headed for eternal death are not warned?

Note: we have indicated that there are many other sins, some of them particularly horrendous; but if a man commits a murder, if he has blood on his hands and all the good things he may have done will not deliver him from the electric chair. How much more severe the punishment or loss may be for those who let people around them go to Hell without a Savior, without warning them, without loving them to Jesus. This too, is called death, the Second Death.

Notice Acts 8, "And Saul was consenting to his death. And at that time there was a great persecution against the church, which was at Jerusalem; and they were all scattered abroad throughout the regions of Judea and Samaria, *except the apostles*" (v. 1). In other words, the authorities, the apostles, the seminary graduates, stayed in Jerusalem.

"Therefore they that were scattered abroad went everywhere preaching the word" (v. 4). Who did this? Primarily a bunch of new converts, or relatively new converts. They declared, shared, proclaimed the word about Jesus. I heard of one translation years ago that said they went about "gossiping" Jesus. That is how the Gospel first spread, and how God would have it spread now.

To maintain that God will see that every man on earth He wants saved will hear the Gospel, and that if one missionary or witness does not go to him, another will go in his place, is skating on very thin theological ice.

Better read what God says through Peter again. *God is not willing that any should perish. He wants all men to be saved.* As do I. I have given my heart, my life, my prayers, and pretty much all I possess to reach lost men and women for Christ.

It was His burning passion for the lost, not mine, that drove me to freeze with my family in wild Alaska, drag logs through the snow out of the woods, to build a church and help build a camp, preach my heart out in hard, tough little villages, live for awhile with no electricity and no water, see my beautiful wife suffer, my daughter get rheumatic fever, be threatened with death by an angry man or two, and yet count it all joy as Christ gave me hundreds of souls for His glory. Thank you, Virginia, my wife, Greg, Rocky and Randy, my sons, and Ginger, my daughter, and especially, thank you Lord Jesus!

God is obviously not willing that any should die without hearing the Gospel, which is why He commissioned us in Mark 16:15, "And he said unto them, Go ye into all the world, and preach the gospel to *every* creature" (emphasis added).

Acts 1:8 also enjoins us, in the passionate parting of Jesus from his followers, "But ye shall receive power after that the Holy Ghost is come upon you; and ye shall be witnesses unto

Chapter Two - Murder In The Church

me both in Jerusalem and in all Judea, and in Samaria, and unto the uttermost part of the earth."

God puts Himself on record that He is not willing "that any should perish." Men are. God is not. "The Lord is not slack concerning his promise, as some men count slackness; but is longsuffering to us-ward, *not willing that any should perish*, but that all should come to repentance" (II Peter 3:9, emphasis added).

How does that square with the teaching that God ordains some men to perish, to go to Hell, but that none He chose to go to Heaven will ever perish? According to this scenario, if a person does not share the Gospel with them, that person may lose their heavenly reward, or suffer some kind of loss, but God will appoint someone to go in their place, so those He wants saved will be saved. In that case, ALL men will be saved, because God does not want ANY to perish. Since we know that millions die without hearing the Gospel, it is either man's fault, or God's fault.

This sets up a comfort zone for the indifferent and unconcerned, as well as for those who would have been witnesses and soul-winners if they had not bought into this philosophy. Not only does this nullify much missionary outreach, it also has a deadening effect on personal witnessing and soul-winning.

The idea is generally that the Will of God cannot be thwarted. This must mean that God's will was being done when men, women, and children perished in the flood. It must mean that the scores of times He implored the children of Israel to turn back to Him, and grieved over their sin and idolatry, He should have been rejoicing because His perfect will was being done.

Such verses as Ezekiel 33 become an exercise in sophistry, or sheer hypocrisy, if God's will can never be thwarted. "Say unto them, As I live, saith the Lord God, I have no pleasure in the death of the wicked, but that the wicked turn from his way and live; turn ye, turn ye from your evil ways, for why will ye die, 0 house of Israel?" (v. 11). Obviously, they died because He did not push the "irresistible grace" button, *and He knew that, so why did He ask?* If they died lost, wasn't that His perfect will? They were not chosen, or elect, or predestined, or *they would have turned to Him, and God knew that.* That is the conclusion if this doctrine is true. That puts this doctrine on very unstable ground.

In I Timothy 2:4, God says, "Who will have all men to be saved, and to come unto the knowledge of the truth." *That* is God *declared* will in His Word. Therefore, let us who love Him carry out His will by His grace, and win precious hellbound souls to the Lord Jesus Christ. Now!

In Matthew 24:37, we hear the broken-hearted lament of Jesus over Jerusalem, "O Jerusalem, Jerusalem, thou that killeth the prophets, and stonest them which are sent unto thee, how often would I have gathered thy children together, even as a hen gathereth her chickens under her wings, and ye would not!"

Notice, the Lord Jesus Christ, God in the flesh, said in essence that it was His will that Jerusalem's children be ga-

Chapter Two - Murder In The Church

thered unto Him, *but they would not. Notice also that His (Jesus) will was thwarted.*

Jesus wept over Jerusalem, their sinful condition, their blindness, and their bitter end. "And when he was come near, he beheld the city, and wept over it . . ." (Luke 19:41). Jesus never contradicted God the Father. Their will was as one. Do you think He was weeping because God's perfect will was being done in Jerusalem? Absolutely not. He was weeping because it was NOT being done.

We can get out of this enigmatic dilemma by saying God's permissive, but not His perfect, will was being done.

Actually, God's will is being done when men use their free will to deny Him, or accept Him, since He gave them that choice. That is in the overall picture. But it breaks His heart, as it broke the heart of Jesus, when men refused Him, so that is NOT His perfect will, His heart's desire. He is "not willing that any should perish," remember?

However, in the sense that God knew all things from eternity, and made provision for them, in the sense that He gave man free will to accept or deny Him, then it is true that His overall will cannot be thwarted, even though He gave them free will to reject His bona fide offer of eternal life.

Men die and go to Hell first of all because they are sinners, as we all are outside of Christ. Many go to Hell because no one told them Christ could free them from their sins, and died for them because He loves them. Men <u>do</u> go to Hell because they do not hear the Gospel.

Either that or it is God's perfect will that they do not hear; He wants them to go to Hell, He chose for them to go to Hell, He does not want them to get the light of Jesus. Could it be that men will spend eternity in Hell because God, who is LOVE, <u>chose</u> for them to spend eternity in the Lake of Fire? Yet He told us to go to all the world and give the gospel to every creature.

I personally believe it is man's failure, not God's choice. Oh yes, I have read the heavy works on the subject by authors such as Lorraine Boettner, Arthur Pink, and James White, and have had friendly discussions with a number of Seminary professors. I have read some of the works of Augustine and John Calvin. I read all the way through Strong's *Systematic Theology* a few months after I was saved, at age 24. I am not saying I am sure I have all the answers. It does mean though, that I am not ignorant of both points of view. I did read God's Word diligently and prayed for the Holy Spirit to open up the Word and the Truth to me, and I believe He did.

Not witnessing is indeed an egregious sin, although other sins may be "just as bad or worse," pride, envy, jealousy, adultery, hatred, lust, immorality, legalism, judgmentalism, drunkenness, covetousness, lying, stealing, but we dare not obfuscate God's mighty blast against those who do not warn the wicked. It is of those, depicted by the watchman of Ezekiel, 33:8-11, even though an exact parallel is not given in the N.T., that God declares that they have blood on their hands. Since a principle is involved, it is a suitable illustration for Christians who do not warn the lost.

Chapter Two – Murder In The Church

I gave a message many years ago, in a great movement of God, in Homer, Ninilchik, and Anchor Point, Alaska. I stated that we were either soul-winners, or soul-murderers. A man named Jim took umbrage at that message. He could not stand the thought of being a soul-murderer, and doubted the scriptural authenticity of such an assertion.

God nevertheless broke Jim's heart, as He did many others in those wild and wonderful days on the Kenai Peninsula, in Alaska. He worked in a filling station for another man and his wife that I had led to Christ. Jim began to ask people if they were saved, if they knew for sure that, if they were to die, they would go to Heaven and not to Hell. There was not much in the way of positive response, at first.

Then one day a salesman made the long drive down from Anchorage to Anchor Point, where the filling station was located. Jim asked him if he was saved, if he knew Jesus. The salesman was shocked! He said he had been thinking about that night and day, and wondered how to be saved. God was dealing with him. Poor Jim got so excited he said he couldn't even find the book of Romans, and wound up somewhere in Isaiah. He led this heartsick sinner to the Lord Jesus Christ, and that started a fire in his soul. Eventually, I was told, he went back to Maryland, and started a church to win more men and women to Jesus Christ!

We sentence men to death, or life imprisonment, for the murder of another man, or men. That is for physical death. How much worse is the murder of a man or men spiritually, when we could have shared with them, or led them to Christ?

To us, it is nothing today in most of our churches. If someone in our church killed somebody, there would be consternation and horror. He would be shunned, and rightly so, and we would consider severe punishment fitting.

Years ago, I read of a fisherman who was fishing on the coast of Florida, I believe. A man was drowning and screaming for help. The fisherman calmly fished while the man drowned, and then when he was through fishing, simply went home. Unfortunately, someone knew about it, and he had to face the consequences.

Imagine letting men and women, boys and girls, go to Hell to burn, in screaming agony, despair, pain, and hopelessness, forever, when we say we have Jesus, the lover of souls in our hearts. We have the power of the glorious Gospel. We have the command of our Savior to love our neighbor as ourselves. We are told to go into all the world and preach the Gospel to every creature. We are guaranteed success with at least some of those with whom we share (see Psalm 126:6).

Our churches may be virtually silent on the subject. Or, they may pay lip service to witnessing; soul-winning. A few may actually be passionate about winning souls, and wonder of wonders, in this age of benign neglect, put soul-winning first!

Look around you! Are you surrounded by people who let other people go to the Lake of Fire without a Savior, without warning them, while they sing, "Oh, How I love Jesus!" Are you a true witness, a soul-winner?

Chapter Two – Murder In The Church

If not, what is the excuse you hide behind? Are you afraid to offend? That is a legitimate concern. In my eagerness, I have pressured some people, thinking they were ready when they were not. I have gone to their houses too often, trying to get them to follow through when they say they have accepted Christ, and they lie about what they said they would do, and will not follow through in obeying Jesus. Sometimes I am afraid I have tried to do the Holy Spirit's work for Him. I have not always been sensitive to their concerns. I have contended earnestly for the faith, as commanded, but perhaps unwittingly at times, I have become contentious, which is ungodly, and forbidden.

Many people are better, sweeter, more sensitive, soul-winners than I. Even some I have led to Christ, or trained to witness, have led hundreds or thousands to Christ. I have to remind myself constantly that God says, "And whosoever shall offend one of these little ones that believe in me, it is better for him that a millstone were hanged about is neck, and he were cast into the sea" (Mark 9:42). I have without fail apologized to those I have offended, if I knew about it, even if I knew in my heart that what they said I said or did was an exaggeration, or even an outright lie! Sometimes it was just my stupid bungling, not listening to the loving, tender voice of God's Holy Spirit. Then I had to weep and pray before God in repentance. I do not want any soul on earth to die and go to Hell because of my offending them!

Having said all of that, and meaning it, no matter how discouraged or heart-broken I have been over my sometimes ineptness, I just ask forgiveness of God and man, and ask Jesus to burn His passion for the lost into my soul, and keep on witnessing! By His grace, I have led thousands to Christ that would otherwise have been lost if I had listened to those who are constantly not witnessing because they are afraid they will offend! While that is a legitimate concern, as I have said, it is much overplayed by the Devil. It is one of his trump cards.

The cross does offend, no matter how softly and gently you present it! Showing proud people that they have broken God's law and are guilty before God, that they are lost sinners, and that the Lord Jesus Christ alone can save them, convicts some, delights some, and offends others.

Jesus, the sweetest, gentlest, most sensitive, loving witness who ever lived, was crucified by those He offended! Let us seek to win souls in His great love, and do our best by His Holy Spirit, to speak the truth in love to the lost. If offense comes, and it surely will to some, let it not be by our obnoxious personality, our witnessing in the flesh, our faltering presentation, but only by the cross!

Sadly, many pastors, where I have had evangelistic meetings all over America, have been embarrassed to go out knocking on doors for Christ. Some have told me, "They will think we are Jehovah's Witnesses, or Mormons!" So I have often gone alone. Why leave the field open to the Devil?

This is not to disparage many godly pastors, evangelists, teachers, missionaries, and Christians in general! They are my very favorite people! How many wonderful, godly pastors

Chapter Two – Murder In The Church

I have prayed with, wept with, counseled with. How many have taught me, and comforted me, as well as fed their congregations and me. Some of them are among my best friends. They are God's special under-shepherds of the sheep. Many of them win more people to Christ on both a yearly and lifetime basis than their whole congregation, which is a bittersweet truth!

Yet, my pastor friends, I have heard some of you greatly emphasize not offending someone as if it was the unpardonable sin, while letting soul-neglecting "Christians" sit comfortably in your pews, congratulating themselves that they have not offended anyone! However, they have offended God by letting souls go to Hell all around them.

Oftentimes, the pastor has aided and abetted their cowardly decisions, by warning and warning them not to offend, and admonishing them when they do! It would have helped so much, if you had comforted them and encouraged them, taught them how to witness better, and given them (and not the complaining sinner) the benefit of the doubt! And consider this; the world certainly has no qualms about offending Christians!

"Christians" afraid to witness, and sinners afraid to completely cut loose and trust and obey Jesus with all their hearts, have a very serious problem. We can plead being shy, timid, inarticulate, inadequate, fearful, or whatever we please, but this is what God says, "But the *fearful*, and unbelieving, and the abominable, and murderers, and whoremongers, and sorcerers [Pharmakkos: an adjective signifying 'devoted to magical arts,' is used as a noun, 'a sorcerer,' especially one who used drugs, potions, spells, enchantments. (*Vines Expository Dictionary*)], idolaters, and all liars, shall have their part in the lake which burneth with fire and brimstone: which is the second death" (Revelation 21:8, emphasis added).

To be too fearful to obey God is eternally fatal! Millions have died for Him, been burned at the stake for Him, endured loss of home and loved ones, and yet some today are afraid to go forward before a friendly church, confess Him as Lord and Savior, and follow Him in baptism, as He commanded. That is not faith, it is fear!

Look at the cross, and the beatings and bloody wounds of Jesus, the Creator/Redeemer of the Universe, who loved you so much He died for you, in your place! He wanted to save you from Hell, from your sins, and bring you to the glorious, indescribable beauty of Heaven, to be with Him, with no suffering or sorrow, or pain or death, but joy forever! He just asks you to give up your doomed and damned life, blighted by sin, for His life, lived in and through you, until He takes you to Heaven!

I repeat, as David Livingston, missionary to dark Africa, who is reputed to have walked 29,000 miles through almost impenetrable jungles to reach lost men and women for Christ, said, "If Christ be God, and died for me, then no Sacrifice is too much to make for Him." Amen!

In the book of Acts, we find the antidote for fear, which is being filled with the Holy Spirit and subsequently speaking boldly for the Lord Jesus Christ! (See Acts 4:8-13). "And

Chapter Two – Murder In The Church

when they had prayed, the place was shaken where they were assembled together; and they were all filled with the Holy Ghost, and they spake the word of God with boldness" (Acts 4:31).

I encouraged some to become soul-winners, sometimes, outstanding soul-winners. Some quit. God help them! And God help the lost souls they could have won to the Lord Jesus Christ.

I have taken any number of soul-winning courses, and taught a number of courses myself. This includes a Personal Evangelism course, the Four-Spiritual Laws course, taught to my church and me by Bill Bright in person. The list of courses also includes Friendship Evangelism, Evangelism Explosion (one of my favorites), *Soul-winning Made Easy*, by C.S. Lovett, and *The Golden Path to Successful Soul-winning*, by John R. Rice. I have read and enjoyed some of George W. Truett's insights, and some of the blessed insights of the author of *With Christ after the Lost* (Scarborough).

I read a superb book, *Great Personal Soul-winners I Have Known*, and marveled at the different approaches God allowed them to use in winning people to Christ. Others include D.L. Moody, Peter Cartwright, Laidlaw, R.A. Torrey, *Life Style Evangelism,* by Joseph Aldrich (I took this course from him personally), Bill Faw, his teaching video, and so many more. I also developed my own simple method of soul-winning. See my newly released book, *So Send I You.*

Anyone with the love of the Lord Jesus Christ in his heart, from a brand new convert, to a hoary old theological genius, can win people to Jesus Christ!

There are approaches that may be too shallow, but God may use them in certain circumstances, with certain people. Some years ago as I lay in the hospital after a heart attack, waiting for a heart transplant, in pain and suffering, and most terrible of all, gasping and fighting for breath, a nurse walked into my room. I was shaking all over and did not even want to speak, yet struggled to get the strength to say, "Have you ever asked the Lord Jesus Christ to come into your heart and save you from your sins?"

"No."

"Would you like to?"

"Yes."

We prayed a brief prayer, recognizing Jesus Christ as Lord, thanking Him for His shed blood on the cross and His resurrection, and she asked Him to forgive her sins and come into her heart and life. After reviewing a few Scriptures, she said she knew that she was saved.

In retrospect, I am not even sure I told her this much, and I collapsed as soon as she left the room, but with inner joy. I do not recommend this approach, but I believe God honored it under these circumstances. It is apparent that His Holy Spirit had already been convicting her of her sins and her lost soul, as was the case of the Philippians jailer in Acts 16.

Some soul-winning courses teach how to win souls without an argument, some advise taking weeks or even months

Chapter Two - Murder In The Church

of cultivating and winning the person's friendship before sharing the Gospel in what should be a receptive heart. Some are bold and hard-hitting, while some are so hung up on love; it takes them forever to get around to sharing the truth. Some are so bent on harsh condemnation that many may recoil. (Remember, we are just beggars sharing Gospel bread with other beggars!) Some believe in Bible Studies with a prospect until God softens his heart. *Disciple Evangelism,* by Kenneth Stephens, is excellent for this, as is my son, Randy McElveen's, *Matriculation Study.*

Some of the great soul-winners in history were very forceful, dragging people out of haystacks, chasing them into their homes. I am thinking of Mordecai Ham and D.L. Moody! I knew of one young preacher who was told that the burly blacksmith beat up every preacher who ever came to his town, and then ran them off. So he went right to the blacksmith, told him he was the new preacher in town and was ready to take his beating. (But he had no intention of leaving.) The blacksmith hit him hard on one cheek and then pounded him on the other cheek, and the young man took it! (Again, not recommended, but God used it; especially when the young man slugged the blacksmith, sat on his chest, and led him to Jesus.)

In some ways, we have frightened people away from winning souls <u>by awakening their fears instead of their faith</u>. Paul argued and disputed daily in the school of one Tyrannus for several years. He was one of the great soul-winners of all time! Jesus called the religious but lost Pharisees of His day "vipers" (essentially, a bunch of snakes). Peter called the devout but lost Jews gathered at Pentecost "murderers," because they had crucified Jesus, the Messiah.

I am by no means suggesting using harsh or abusive language with those we are witnessing to about Christ. I am trying to counter the pervasive overkill permeating many of our churches about "offending!" Constantly, prayerfully, seek to speak the truth in love, the love of the Lord Jesus Christ through you! Let us avoid a truculent attitude, by all means. Let us also avoid the almost obsequious manner of some in presenting Christ, as if we were apologizing for doing so!

Consider the following illustration. One horrible night, lightning strikes fields and forests all around a city of about a million people. Fires begin to burn all over the city. Swirling winds begin to blow, and the fire races upon the unsuspecting sleeping people. Alarms, desperate phone calls, and pleas for help pour into the main fire station. Here and there, now and then, a fireman runs to the fire pole, slides down, and gets a few others to go with him to fight the fire and rescue people. But the great majority of the many firemen in this gigantic model fire station never go into action. The fire ravages the city with the ferocity of a demon from Hell! Tens of thousands die. Most of the city lies in ruins. The stench of burning flesh, the screams of agony, fear and dying, the loss of homes and possessions, is incredible.

As time goes on, the outrage simmering in the hearts of the survivors bursts into full flame! They demand a court trial, open to all, of the recalcitrant firemen. Many clamor loud-

Chapter Two - Murder In The Church

ly for the death penalty on them all, with the exception of the few who responded to help. (Some of those few paid with their lives as they heroically fought the huge fire.)

When they were allowed to speak, the facts came out. Some had been drinking and were too drunk to perform their duties, or even comprehend the magnitude of the threat. Others were playing poker. Several were looking at pornographic magazines. There were some who were involved in cleaning the fire station and checking the readiness of the fire trucks. One man was conducting a Bible study with several of his fellow firemen. Four were playing table tennis. Several were under the influence of drugs, and too euphoric to understand the danger. Another was studying the instruction book for firemen, and trying to learn how to be a better fireman. Finally, several more were in a prayer meeting for the city, as they saw and heard the great calamity.

What is the point? When the verdict was given, all were equally condemned! Whether they were doing something good or something bad was immaterial. They incurred the hatred and contempt of the city, and of the court. They earned their condemnation! They did not do the very heart of their calling as firemen, to put out fires, to rush to their goal, leaving all else behind, to rescue dear, endangered people from a terrible death! And there, my friend, you have a parable of the Church and the Christians of today!

The fires of Hell are moving upon lost human beings. Every human being is just one heartbeat from Hell, and the

Lake of Fire, if he or she does not come to know the Lord Jesus Christ.

Christians are <u>commanded</u> to reach the lost. Christians are <u>commissioned</u> to reach the lost. Christians are <u>empowered</u> to reach the lost. Christians are <u>implored</u> to reach the lost!

Jesus did not leave all His passion for souls on the cross. The same Christ who died on bloody Calvary now lives in true Christian's hearts. He dwells by His Holy Spirit in their body, as His Temple. His burning, consuming passion that sent Him to the torturous, excruciating pain and bloody death on the cross for sinners still pours from His burdened heart, and He now indwells us. How can we not have a passion for souls? His passion demands expression through us. Let Him love a lost world through us!

The very heart of our calling to the salvation of the Lord Jesus Christ, once we are saved, is to share Him. All else is a tributary to the mighty rushing river of His love for souls!

Shortly after I was saved, I was driving down a street in Gladstone, Oregon, with my magnificent pastor, Dr. Herb Anderson. We were heading to the church for a service. I commented on a group of youth playing softball. I said, "They should be in church," thinking that softball was keeping them from church. Dr. Herb Anderson taught me a lesson I have never forgotten.

The gist of what he had to say was that it was really good that they were playing softball and not out drinking or partying. It was a healthy, clean sport, and they were having a great deal of normal fun. Then he looked at me and said,

Chapter Two – Murder In The Church

"Mac, always remember that the good is the enemy of the best!"

How true that is in our churches! We have dozens of programs, every one of them good, or serving some good purpose. No one would dare attack any one of those programs, as someone is being helped, taught, or encouraged by them. Many of us are racing from meeting to meeting, until we are exhausted, "doing the work of the Lord."

What if we wiped out about 90 percent of the meetings, and concentrated on serious Bible study, prayer, and training, and encouraged every Christian to call on the lost, and made time, provision, and leaders to aid them in doing just that?

There was a time when churches held all-night prayer meetings, and wept for the lost. Most churches today do not even have prayer meetings, though the name is still used. We have Bible studies, with just a little prayer. Here and there, several people may pray together regularly, but if so, they do it pretty much on their own!

Much of our teaching is in the form of lectures. There is a time and place for that, as we can see from some of Jesus' teaching in the Word of God. Yet Jesus taught as much or more by discussion, question and answer, and telling stories, parables, and illustrations, and then using questions to see if the listeners understood Him. Then He explained His illustrations. It was give and take, and people participated, and stayed awake.

In Thessalonica, Paul reasoned (verb form, dialegomai) with them, conducted a discussion with them out of the Scriptures, for three Sabbaths. "For three Sabbaths reasoned with them from the Scriptures, explaining and giving evidence that the Christ had to suffer and rise again from the dead" (Acts 17:2-3). He did exactly the same thing in Corinth and Ephesus. This was no aberration; it was his normal method of teaching.

Not too long ago, I checked on a very good Bible teacher, who had taught for about 10 years with the lecture method. He was brilliant, and often fascinating. However, I conducted a small survey with about 47 people; most, if not all, of whom had been under his excellent teaching. Only 11 read their Bibles daily, many lapsed in other Christian expressions of faith, and few, if any, were practicing winning souls.

I use Greek, and sometimes Hebrew, study tools, and love them. Thank God for those brilliant and dedicated expositors who study indefatigably so common folks like me can find and understand the truth, especially of difficult passages. Yet I see no evidence that Jesus and His disciples sat around parsing the Greek and Hebrew in language studies interminably!

Remember, if scholars are correct, they used the Septuagint, a translation of the Hebrew Scriptures into the Greek language, deciphered by 70 Jewish Scholars about 200 years before the coming of Jesus Christ! (These are round figures; sometimes the number of Jews and the number of years vary slightly, but not enough to matter).

Jesus opened their understanding, and helped them with puzzling portions of Scripture, but hardly seems to have

Chapter Two - Murder In The Church

taught through any book of the Bible verse by verse! Read how He taught.

I have often taught through books of the Bible verse by verse, and thoroughly enjoyed it. But it seems to me that this over-emphasis may have eclipsed other great methods of teaching. The average Christian knows that Jesus Christ is God, but most would find it difficult, if not impossible, to prove it from Scripture! That is tragic! This is fundamental to any idea of salvation, and to any real growing in grace, and in the knowledge of our Lord and Savior, Jesus Christ.

It also makes it hard for them to reach the lost, and impossible to reach the dedicated cultist who denies the Deity of the Lord Jesus Christ. This means that something is badly flawed in our method of teaching, or in the content of our teaching. This is only one example; there are many. It also sets professing Christians up to be won by the cultists to their false religion, and Mormons and Jehovah's Witnesses flourish with the thousands of "Christians" they have won to their kingdom of darkness.

Yet we must remember that God's Word says, "But the natural man receiveth not the things of the Spirit of God; for they are foolishness to him: neither can he know them, because they are spiritually discerned" (II Corinthians 2:14).

The unsaved man cannot understand the Bible until he is saved. He can understand that he is a sinner, and that Christ died for his sins on the cross. He can understand that he will spend eternity in Heaven or Hell, depending on what he does with Jesus. For that reason, he cannot understand the Bible, even if he is a college or Seminary professor! The historical parts, yes. The spiritual content, absolutely not!

It takes the Author of the Book, the Holy Spirit, dwelling in him, to open his mind to understand the Bible! It does not matter how much dynamic equivalence we offer the unsaved man in Bible translations. He still will not be able to understand the Word of God. We have thought that it was the stilted English, or archaic words of the King James Bible, that kept the sinner from understanding the Word of God, or modern Christians from studying the Bible, but that is proving not to be so! True, we need to bring the archaic words up to date, without doing violence to the text.

I am not against translations, and I have used many of them, yet I have noticed a strange anomaly. Actually, people were much more Biblically literate, when we had only two or three outstanding versions of the Bible, than they are now with hundreds of translations. Dynamic equivalence seeks to clarify what God is saying, when the words in the Hebrew or Greek cannot be translated exactly by matching words in English. Therefore, what God is actually saying and what He means may require dynamic equivalence. There may simply not be an English word to translate literally, the exact, same, Greek word.

What many dynamic equivalent translation versions do is to seek each one to make the Bible even clearer. That is a noble and wonderful endeavor. Unfortunately, many are building on the thoughts of other translations trying to do the same. Sometimes, this results in getting ever further from the

Chapter Two - Murder In The Church

very Word of God! Moreover, it becomes even more difficult to quote the Word of God, and listen to others quote the Word of God, with so many differences, and that is a shame! God is not the author of confusion!

Furthermore, Revelation 22:18-19, is still in the Book!

For I testify unto every man that heareth the words of the prophecy of this book, If any man shall add unto these things, God shall add unto him the plagues that are written in this book: And if any man shall take away from the words of this prophecy, God shall take away his part out of the book of life, and out of the holy city, and from the things which are written in this book.

What a thunderous and ominous warning! And God means it! Do not mess with the words of the Word of God! For a classic book on this subject, which I believe will rock and change the whole translation world within the next 20 years, get and read *The Word of God in English*, by Leland Ryken. This book is highly recommended by Dr. John MacArthur, Dr. Gordon Wenham, Dr. Wayne Grudem, Dr. Bruce Ware, Dr. J.I. Packer, and others, including me!

Another thing contributing to confusion in the Church is the use of psychological words and concepts as if they were Scriptural. Pastors and Bible teachers, and many books, still speak highly of self-esteem, (esteeming one's self) when actually Jesus spoke instead of denying oneself! "And He said to them all, If any man will come after me, let him deny himself, and take up his cross daily, and follow me" (Luke 9:23). Tests have shown that criminals generally have better self-esteem than the general public!

Others are still hooked on getting people to "love themselves." They may quote Matthew, which is teaching the very opposite of what they say. Jesus said unto him, "Thou shalt love the Lord thy God with all thy heart, and with all thy soul, and with all thy mind. This is the first and great commandment. And the second is like unto it, Thou shalt love thy neighbour as thyself, on these two commandments hang all the law and the prophets" (22:37-40).

There are only two commandments here, not three. The two are to love God, and to love thy neighbor. There is absolutely no command to love ourselves. That is our problem, not our solution. We love ourselves too much. He knows we love ourselves. He just commands us to love our neighbor *as much* as we love ourselves! Loving ourselves is a given. If we really do that, and salvation is the greatest and most wonderful thing that has ever happened to us, and the love of Jesus has transformed our lives, we cannot help but share Him with our neighbor—if we love him as we love ourselves!

Psychology has wrested and distorted that idea, and many Christian leaders have fallen into that trap, thinking it to be Scriptural, when it is anything but Scriptural.

In spite of earnest teaching by many godly pastors (and almost all of the pastors I know are hard-working, godly men, feeding and often weeping for their congregations), in the average congregation, on an average Sunday morning, more

Chapter Two – Murder In The Church

members of the congregation stay home than go to church! Try that in a business, and then try to run the business. Try that on a football team, and then try to win games! Try that in an army, with a formidable foe massed for battle.

We are in a stupendous battle to the death for the souls of men and women, boys and girls, for the Lord Jesus Christ. To ignore, or show contempt for the church, reveals the true condition of the professing Christian's heart.

Christ claimed that He is the Head of the church, and the church is His body. To be married to the Head, and yet not to the body, the church, exposes the fatal delusion of many "Christians" who show little interest in, or loyalty to, the local church. It clearly violates the very essence of the love that proves one a Christian. "We know that we have passed from death unto life, because we love the brethren. He that loveth not his brother abideth in death" (I John 3:14).

Church is where we meet regularly to share with those brothers we love, study the word, grow in grace, love and encourage one another, use our spiritual gifts, and reach out to a lost world together for Christ. God established the church, and to ignore it is an insult to God. He said clearly in His Word:

Not forsaking the assembling of ourselves together, as the manner of some is, but exhorting one another, and so much the more as ye see the day approaching (Hebrews 10:25).

By this shall all men know that ye are my disciples, if ye have love one to another (John 13:35).

We are also in a gargantuan battle for professing Christians, to make sure they are (1) really saved, (2) growing in grace and in the knowledge of our Lord and Savior, Jesus Christ, (3) sharing Christ effectively by life and lip, (4) exercising their spiritual gifts, (5) identifying the culture of this pagan world, and standing against it, (6) baptized with the love of God for Jesus, the Bible, for Christians, for the Church, and for the lost, and (7) living a life of victory over sin, the world, the flesh, and the devil.

I have mentioned previously things that may be contributing to the rampant unbelief, dereliction of duty, desertion, and lack of loyalty plaguing the Church. Here is a short list:

- The lack of using the Ten Commandments to produce conviction of sin. The proper use of the Ten Commandments will result in people realizing that they are lost, hopeless, before a Holy God.
- The lack of preaching on Judgment, on Hell, and man's imminent doom.
- The wicked immorality of the World invading the church.
- The lack of solid, powerful preaching on sin.
- The ecumenical shredding of doctrinal truth, in unholy alliances with apostate churches.

- The weakening of the Bible message by a superfluity of dynamic equivalent translations, and by liberal attacks on the inspired, infallible, inerrant, Word of God, often disguised as "scholarship."

We have conservative scholars, such as Josh McDowell, and many other astute theologians, with whom the "Jesus Seminar," and other liberal deniers of the Bible, would not dare debate! The universities, and now some colleges and high schools, belittle the Bible, and advance evolution, a myth "intellectuals" love to play with.

No matter what happens, there will always be a godly, though perhaps bitterly, persecuted remnant of Christians and Churches, as there was of the Jews, when God's judgment fell on them. Yet He has not totally forsaken His chosen people, the Jews, whom He foreknew, and He will not utterly forsake us. However, His wrath may soon be unleashed upon us for our rebellion, worldliness, unbelief, brutal murder of millions of precious babies, and rampant immorality. Our present economic distress may be only a small precursor of what is soon coming.

"Even so, come, Lord Jesus" (Revelation 22:20b).

The Late Great American Church

Bloody Hands, Broken Hearts and Lost Souls

If thou forbear to deliver them that are drawn unto death, and those that are ready to be slain; If thous sayest, Behold, we knew it not; doth not he that pondereth the heart consider it? and he that keepeth thy soul, doth not he know it? and shall not he render to every man according to his works? (Proverbs 24:11-12)

We have quoted Ezekiel 33:8, "When I say unto the wicked, O wicked man, thou shalt surely die; if thou dost not speak to warn the wicked from his way, that wicked man shall die in his iniquity; but his blood will I require at thine hands." Look also at verse 9, "Nevertheless, if thou warn the wicked of his way to turn from it; if he do not turn from his way, he shall die in his iniquity; but thou hast delivered thy soul."

Warning the wicked is top priority with God, and we are the watchmen He has commissioned and commanded to do just that! To those who do not warn the wicked, the consequences are horrendous. Blood required at their hands. Murder by callous neglect.

How serious a sin is this, according to God Himself? Serious enough that He says of those who do warn the wicked, even if the wicked do not repent, that the witness of you, the watchman, hast delivered thy soul! How would you like to face God with blood to be required at your hands, because you did not warn lost sinners of their true condition, and give them the good news of Jesus, so that they could be saved, and not spend eternity in Hell? How would you like to face God if you do not warn the lost, and you have not delivered your soul?

As I have considered this portion in preaching as an evangelist in the past, I have also connected it with Matthew 7:13-14, "Enter ye in at the strait gate: for wide is the gate, and broad is the way, that leadeth to destruction, and many there be which go in thereat: Because strait is the gate, and narrow is the way, which leadeth unto life, and few there be that find it."

God gave the flaming torch of evangelism and His love to the Jews to be a light unto the Gentiles. Speaking to His chosen nation of Israel, the Jews, God said, "I the Lord have called thee in righteousness, and will hold thine hand, and will keep thee, and give thee for a covenant of the people, for a light of the Gentiles. . ." (Isaiah 42:6).

As Israel, led by God, conquered the people of Canaan and brought down mighty kingdoms and many Kings, God put them in position to share Him with the Gentile world. Some Gentiles did find the light of the Lord Jehovah through the Jewish people down through the centuries, but again and again they wandered from God in rebellion, even after scores of warnings from God through His prophets, both major and minor.

Chapter Three - Bloody Hands, Broken Hearts and Lost Souls

Essentially, they departed from their main purpose as a chosen people, to know, obey, and love the Lord, and to share Him with all the Gentiles (nations: anyone not a Jew is a Gentile).

As I contemplated this, and noted the warnings given over centuries to Israel, I remembered that God finally turned from Israel to the Gentiles, because of Israel's sin and rebellion, and idolatry, and most particularly because they ceased to be a light unto the Gentiles and evangelize them. The result of God's taking His hand off them was their prophesied scattering throughout the whole world, the intense persecution that has decimated and destroyed them down through the centuries, the million or more Jews killed in Jerusalem in 70 A.D. and climaxed by the Holocaust, where six million men, women and children were systematically tortured, starved, and slaughtered by Germany under Hitler.

They did fulfill God's prophecy for them, in that they returned to their homeland and re-established their nation after 2,500 years, miraculously, declaring themselves a nation again on May 14, 1948. Yet the nation remains estranged from God, with only some individual Jews here and there coming to the Messiah.

God then called out His church, and called on them (us) to go into all the world and preach the Gospel to every creature. He is the Light of the world, but now He has commissioned us as light-bearers, to share the Gospel faithfully. We seem to be in about the same position now that the Jews were in when He turned from them! Is most of the Church now on the "broad" way? I hope not.

One of Billy Graham's subjects in college was anthropology, the study of man and his origins, culture, religion, etc. He said that man is incurably religious, since 95 percent of all races, nations and cultures have some kind of a god! Yet all the "gods" in the world cannot save one soul. That is why Jesus Christ came to redeem and ransom us by His shed blood on the cross.

The people of Noah's day undoubtedly had "religion," but, according to some calculations, they had 120 years of warning by Noah that judgment was coming! "And God saw that the wickedness of man was great in the earth, and that every imagination of the thoughts of his heart was only evil continually" (Genesis 6:5). They scoffed and refused the salvation of the ark, and the flood mercilessly drowned them all, men, women, and children. Only the eight souls on the ark were saved out of all of what could have been millions, according to some population experts.

How many were saved from the sizeable cities of Sodom and Gomorrah? Only four, and one of those looked back against God's command, and perished. (Lot, his wife, and two daughters. His wife looked back, and perished.)

Is it just possible that we are so blinded that we believe that since America is so religious, history will not repeat itself with us who are Christians, or professing Christians, and with America itself? It has always been the few, the remnant, that are saved when God sorts the wheat from the chaff and

Chapter Three - Bloody Hands, Broken Hearts and Lost Souls

judgment comes! Are the great masses of America's professing Christianity really on the "broad way" to Hell?

Perhaps the surest sign that we have lost our way, that Christians and the Church are in big trouble, is not just our sins, awful as they are against a Holy God, but that we have lost our way, and forgotten the goal. Our apathy toward a lost world is inexcusable. Imagine, only two to three percent of professing Christians *ever* lead anyone to Christ. This is the scandal of Christianity today.

Those of us who have seen photos, or movies, or have actually seen the holocaust horrors where six million Jews, were starved, tortured, submitted to horrible sex acts in rape and homosexual attacks, enslaved, hauled to incarceration and death in stinking box cars, used for medical experimentation, put into gas chambers, stripped and marched out to be shot and pushed into open graves, are horrified that we humans could be so wicked, but we certainly are, outside of Jesus Christ.

Though it is possible that only a small percentage of the victims knew Jesus Christ, some did. For them, no matter how excruciating the pain and hurt, and how interminably the torture and despair, their death freed them to be with Jesus. How precious! No wonder the Lord says that "Precious in the sight of the Lord is the death of His saints" (Psalm 116:15).

Yet, my dear, beloved fellow Christians, the holocaust at least came to an end. How much more horrible it is to let sinners go to an eternal Hell, with total despair, intense pain, no hope, separation forever from God, burning forever in the

Lake of Fire (see Revelation 20:11-15) without doing everything possible to win them to Jesus! But, that is *not* the burning passion igniting the hearts of 97 percent of those who call themselves Christians.

We consider those who performed such heinous atrocities on the Jews as fiends in human flesh.

What about us?

In Matthew, Jesus gave a crystal clear declaration, "And he saith unto them, Follow me and I will make you fishers of men" (4:19). Are we really following Jesus, if we are not fishing for men? Did Jesus lie? (Perish the thought . . . impossible, but we act as if He did.)

Consider this similar verse, "And they said, Believe on the Lord Jesus Christ, and thou shalt be saved. . ." (Acts 16:31). Many, including the Philippian jailer to whom these words were given, have confidently staked their eternity on this pungent truth.

How can we say we believe on the Lord Jesus Christ, therefore we are saved, as this verse clearly teaches, but only pretend we are following Jesus, because we are not fishing for souls, even though the verse in Matthew 4:19 assuredly declares that we who follow Him will be fishers of men?

At times, pastors or church leaders have taken me aside, and said something like this, "Now, Brother Mac, we believe in witnessing, and soul-winning, but there is much more to the Christian life than soul-winning. There is the command to grow in grace, and be conformed to the image of Christ; we are admonished to *study the word*, we are told to *pray without*

Chapter Three - Bloody Hands, Broken Hearts and Lost Souls

ceasing, and we need to know *how to love one another*, the sure mark of a Christian. We need to use our spiritual gifts in the body of Christ, worship God in spirit and in truth, praise Him, rejoice in Him, encourage our brothers and sisters in the faith, feed the poor, eschew sin, live godly lives, flee temptation and have an intimate personal relationship with Jesus Christ. We believe in balance in our Christian lives!"

Balance? Almost 98 percent of professing Christians *never* lead anyone to Christ. That is rebellious disobedience to the Will of God and to the Word of God.

Almost every Christian will come out to a fun night with food and fellowship, and an interesting, entertaining night at the church! Many will come out to play basketball, softball, volleyball or soccer at the church. However, attendance on "calling night" to reach out to the lost in the average church is dismal! Few come, and most of them do not last. Calling night for Christ is almost ignored on the church calendar, with anything and everything scheduled on that night, as if it was insignificant, and it soon becomes just that. The night or nights of calling and outreach should be the most important night of the week, or at least as important as any other night.

Sometimes I hear people, pastors, and friends say, "Mac, you don't have to come out to calling night, Tuesday, Thursday, or whatever night is designated, to be a soul-winner!" Of course, you do not. Many, because of age, jobs, sickness, or other considerations, cannot come out on these special nights, yet they can become powerful witnesses, even soul-winners, if they commit themselves unreservedly to reaching lost souls for the Lord Jesus Christ. I deal with many types of outreach in my book, *So Send I You*, and all of us can use some of them. Yet let us face the facts. In scores of churches I have been in, if nights of calling are neglected or eliminated, the soul-winning outreach of that church often plunges dramatically!

A soul-winning, outreach night gives purpose, sets aside a time, encourages fellow Christians, and sometimes transforms a church. I have yet to see many people won to Christ on a steady basis and brought into the church by those who do not honor the outreach night or nights. It can happen, but seldom does. Theory is not fact. Actually, both an outreach night or nights, and daily witnessing by all believers is the ideal. Dear God, revive us to have that kind of church.

The outreach program should be promoted with joy, and new converts won should give their testimony publicly. There should be a continual, not just one shot, training program, to train every Christian how to share Christ. It should be tremendously exciting, with frequent banquets for souls saved, and those who won them, to share testimonies and praise God together! Christians should be trained in discipleship, and all new converts should be discipled, if possible.

In one of the churches I started in Alaska, we had Tuesday morning calling, mostly ladies, though some men came; Tuesday night calling, for men and women; and Thursday night calling for men and women, though mostly men came. Many came to Christ, and some of the callers got so excited about soul-winning they went into full time service for the

Chapter Three – Bloody Hands, Broken Hearts and Lost Souls

Lord! We also had a sports program on Monday, with devotions and invitation.

Sports can be detrimental to the Gospel, often capturing hearts, time, and focus away from the Lord Jesus Christ. I am very thankful to say that the church I am now a member of, Calvary Baptist in Petal, Mississippi, has at least to some degree, nullified this juggernaut of benign malevolence. Led by Pastor Terrell Stringer, and a fine staff of Boyd Tweedy and Charles Tweedy, along with many others in the congregation, our soccer program enlists over a hundred children and youth. Scores of adults attend. This does not even include our T-ball, softball, basketball, etc., and our top-notch Awana program, with its intense evangelistic Bible study and fun activities.

Devotions are given, and visits made to follow up. We are beginning to see a harvest from this outreach. Years of prayer and messages on winning people to Christ, seemingly now is starting to pay off. Some of our people are learning how to lead these young people to Christ, by actual experience.

"Was your church perfect, Brother Mac?" Absolutely not! I made mistakes, and still do. Many churches have better programs, and better soul-winners, than I, Praise the Lord! However, unfortunately, such churches are few and far between these days.

Balance? Yes, let us have balance! Real balance. Rescue soul-winning from the garbage can, where many churches have thrown it, or at the very least, neglected it.

One factor I have not yet emphasized nearly enough in seeing a church and its membership transformed into a dynamic, soul-winning church, permeated with changed lives, holiness and power, is embodied in I John 3:1-3, "Behold, what manner of love the Father hath bestowed upon us that we should be called the sons of God: therefore the world knoweth us not, because it knew him not. Beloved, now are we the sons of God, and it doth not yet appear what we shall be: but we know that, when he shall appear, we shall be like him; for we shall see him as he is. And every man that hath this hope in him purifieth himself, even as he is pure."

Focusing on, longing for, living in light of the soon coming of Jesus Christ for all true believers, will purify us, give us an urgent desire to reach souls, and intensify our love for Jesus. No wonder John, the mighty Apostle, prayed, ". . . Even so, come, Lord Jesus" (Revelation 22:20b).

This event, which Christians call the Rapture, or the catching away of the Church to be with Jesus forever, is embodied in I Thessalonians 4:13-18.

But I would not have you to be ignorant, brethren, concerning them which are asleep, that ye sorrow not, even as others which have no hope. For if we believe that Jesus died and rose again, even so them also which sleep in Jesus will God bring with him, For this we say unto you by the word of the Lord, that we which are alive and remain unto the coming of the Lord shall not prevent them which are asleep. For the Lord himself shall descend from heaven with a shout, with the voice of the archangel, and with the trump of God: and the dead in Christ shall rise first: Then we which are alive and

Chapter Three - Bloody Hands, Broken Hearts and Lost Souls

remain shall be caught up together with them in the clouds, to meet the Lord in the air, and so shall we ever be with the Lord: Wherefore comfort one another with these words.

No other people on the face of the earth have this wonderful, blessed hope, but Christians. What a glorious future!

Some talk about the tenderness and love of God we should show to a community in order to reach them for Christ. Tell them about the wonderful, abundant life Christ promised, and how they can have peace, and joy. Tell them He wants to have an intimate personal relationship with them. He wants to free the alcoholic, the dope addict, the workaholic, the hedonists, the pornographer. Tell them God loves them!

There is a good bit of truth in these assertions. We should walk in love, as we are admonished in Scripture. Incidentally, as far as an approach to lost sinners is concerned, there are two problems, at least, in telling them *first* how much God loves them.

If someone had approached me before I was saved and asked me if I had or wanted an intimate personal relationship with Jesus, I would have certainly thought that I already had that. Even though I had been very immoral in the Navy, and afterward for a while, I had asked forgiveness for that, gotten married to a beautiful Christian girl, attended church and taught Sunday School. Many times, I talked to Jesus, prayed to Him, asked forgiveness when I sinned, etc.

My heart often warmed as I thought of Him. I did believe in His death, burial, and resurrection. But I was *not* a Christian! It took a real shock, and a man of God, named Guy Zehring, who pierced through my façade, with the Word of God, and truly led me to Christ. An "intimate personal relationship" approach would never have worked with me. Guy talked to me about being a sinner, about Hell, about being able to *know* for *sure* that I was saved, and led me to Christ!

Listen to this tale of two doctors.

A man goes to a doctor to be checked for cancer. He is a personal friend of the doctor. To the doctor's surprise and sorrow, his friend has a very advanced form of cancer. Immediate treatment may save his life, but he will have to submit to a very painful operation, chemotherapy, and radiation. When he interviews his friend after the confirming tests, he pats him on the shoulder and says, "Jim, I love you. Go out and enjoy your life, golf, and all that good stuff. Tell your pretty wife hello for me."

The doctor "loves" Jim too much to tell him the unvarnished truth, and so *lovingly* condemns him to death!

Another man in the same city goes to a different doctor. They, too, are friends. The doctor examines his friend Bob, and to his consternation, discovers that Bob has a serious case of cancer that will be terminal shortly, unless aggressively treated.

He says, "Bob, I am your friend, and I love you. It grieves me to tell you that you have advanced cancer, and your only

Chapter Three – Bloody Hands, Broken Hearts and Lost Souls

hope is an immediate operation and continued treatment. Otherwise, you will die."

Which doctor really loves his friend, his cancer patient? The answer is obvious. Love that does not tell the full truth is cowardice, not real love.

Men are sinners, with terminal cancer of the soul. They are lawbreakers before a *Holy God*. They are *lost*! They are in danger of plunging any moment into an eternal Hell. To tell them how much God loves them is to give them the cure before they know they have the disease. This may lead to a decision for Christ, and false assurance, while they are still on the road to Hell. How unutterably tragic! That is one reason why we have so many casual converts, nonchalant about the Christian life, and often pursuing sin as avidly as ever.

When the law of God is used, when sin is thundered forth from the pulpit, when men realize they are sinners both by imputation from Adam, and by nature and choice, when they realize life is a vapor, and Hell is one breath away, <u>then</u> preach the incredible, beautiful, overwhelming love of God. How sweet that love appears, how magnificent, against the background of the judgment we all so richly deserve! Then and then only does the *love of God* burst forth in full bloom, irresistibly attractive to lost, damned, hopeless, condemned sinners! Like a blazing sun appearing in the middle of a black cloud, the sinner's attention is riveted breathlessly on the cross, on grace, on the Lord Jesus Christ, and His bloody sacrifice.

When he flees to the cross and is saved, his gratitude and joy know no bounds! Jesus has saved him from sin, and death, and Hell. He will cry out for all the world to hear, "Oh, Jesus, thank you, thank you, I want to live in gratitude and love for you the rest of my life, and share you with my lost family and friends. Thank you, Lord Jesus, for washing my sins away by your shed blood, for forgiving me, for saving me from sin and Hell, and for giving me everlasting life, and a home in Heaven with you forever!" *That is when* the love of God, the tenderness of a Father, the fellowship of one who said, "I will never leave you or forsake you," should be preached and taught to the exhilarated new believer, and his privileges and responsibilities as a new child of God taught him.

Devoid of the *fear* of God, the *love* of God may degenerate into a pallid imitation of the real thing.

I remember reading of a survey mentioned by the brilliant Dr. James Kennedy, of *Evangelism Explosion* fame, in which he said that the great majority of youth and youth leaders, when asked why they came to Christ, said, "The *fear* of Hell."

What Does The Holy Spirit Use To Bring Men To Christ?

And when they had prayed, the place was shaken where they were assembled together; and they were all filled with the Holy Ghost, and they spake the word of God with boldness (Acts 4:31).

What does the Holy Spirit use to bring men to Christ? The Bible and the Gospel, of course. But, consider carefully the following. When I was a missionary to Alaska, we stopped and ate at Prairie Bible Institute in Alberta, Canada, and I met the godly teacher and principal, L.E. Maxwell. Wonderful!

According to Ray Comfort, L.E. Maxwell wrote of how students came to a knowledge of salvation. Some were "moved by fear" and others were "moved by love." He noted that between 1931 and 1949, of the 2,507 students, nearly 65 percent were moved by fear, and only six percent were moved by love. The remaining 29 percent came with another motive or could not remember why they came to the Savior (*Revival's Golden Key: Unlocking the Door to Revival,* 2002, p. 80*).*

Satan has fought hard to get preaching on Sin and Hell abandoned today, and you can see why! His adroit use of Scripture, even through godly pastors, has furnished the background for this abandonment, which in part accounts for the eviscerated Christianity of today. The sad results are fewer and fewer real converts. Ray Comfort wrote:

As Christians, have they yet come to a point of fearing God? What do they think when they read that God killed a husband and wife because they broke the Ninth Commandment (Acts 5:1-10)? Do they conclude that the psalmist was misguided when he wrote, *"My flesh trembles for fear of You, and I am afraid of your judgments"* (Psalm 119-120)? Have they obeyed the command of Jesus: *"I will show you whom you should fear: Fear Him who, after He has killed, has power to cast into hell; yes, I say to you, fear Him!"* (Luke 12:5)? (p. 87).

God provides a promise for those who do fear Him. *"Blessed is everyone who fears the LORD, who walks in His ways"* (Psalm 128:1).

Comfort also noted:

Psalm 2:11 commands, *"Serve the Lord with fear, and rejoice with trembling."* The early Church did just that; they walked "in the fear of the Lord" (Acts 9:31).

Scripture makes it very clear what it is that causes men to flee from sin. It's the *"fear of the Lord"* (Proverbs 16:6). When F. B. Meyer questioned four hundred Christian workers about why they came to Christ, "an overwhelming number testified that it was because of some message or influence of the terror of the Lord." The famous Bible teacher then

Chapter Four – What Does The Holy Spirit Use To Bring Men To Christ?

said, "Oh, this is more than interesting and astonishing, especially in these days when we are rebuked often for not preaching more of the love of God!" (pp. 87-88).

Comfort adds some information from Bill Bright, of Campus Crusade for Christ International, about thirty-three recorded instances of Jesus speaking about Hell, which probably means He warned of Hell thousands of times. Bright said the Bible refers to Hell a total of 167 times. He added, "To be silent on the eternal destinations of souls is to be like a sentry failing to warn his fellow soldiers of impending attack."

From Alaska to Canada, to California, to Oregon, to Idaho, to Washington, to Michigan, to Massachusetts, and across America, I have preached to reach sinners for Christ, using both the motive of love and the motive of fear. I believe my messages on Hell were some of the most productive in winning souls to Christ.

Paul said, *"And how I kept back nothing that was profitable unto you, but have shewed [showed] you, and have taught you publicly, and from house to house, Testifying both to the Jew and also to the Greeks, repentance toward God, and faith toward our Lord Jesus Christ"* (Acts 20:21). *"Therefore watch, and remember, that by the space of three years, I ceased not to warn every one night and day with tears"* (v. 31). Notice, you do not warn someone about the love of God, but to flee from the wrath of God, and not to ignore, neglect, or despise His love. Note also, that Paul gave such warnings with tears, with a broken heart. I have said repeatedly in my meetings, when I preached on Hell, that no one should preach on Hell without a broken heart. With tears, not vindictiveness, but with God's urgent passion for the lost.

Keep in mind that sinners, dominated by the old sin nature, have little attraction to the love of God, until the fear of God begins to wake them up. The natural, unsaved man may desperately at times want love, but that may mean he wants affection from some fellow human being, consideration, sex, acknowledgement of his worth, attention, or to have his basic needs met. He may want a love that ministers to him, or helps him in his physical or emotional needs. Rarely does it ever mean he is urgently seeking God's love. *"There is none that understandeth, there is none that seeketh after God"* (Romans 3:11).

To water down Hell by telling the unsaved that they may be "separated from God forever" means little to the average sinner, especially one who is enjoying his sins, and enjoying life. He has been separated from God all of his life, and he loves it! He has no idea that every breath he draws, every heartbeat, is solely by the grace of God. He has no idea of the extreme danger he is in every moment day and night, of spending an eternity in Hell, until he is warned, with no mincing of words, but in the love of Christ.

On the contrary, it is true that if a congregation begins to really love one another, and have a continual baptism of the love of Jesus, growing in grace and in the knowledge of our Lord and Savior, Jesus Christ, and gets excited about Him,

Chapter Four – What Does The Holy Spirit Use To Bring Men To Christ?

and the needs around them, and especially the lost, it can act like a magnet to attract the attention and desire of sinners who would not otherwise be interested. These sinners have never encountered anything like that in their dog-eat-dog world, and they begin to have a hunger to see what makes that kind of church, and these kinds of Christians, tick. Faith still comes by hearing, and hearing by the Word of God, but this makes them *want* to hear (see Romans 10:17).

"God loves you and has a wonderful plan for your life," might seem hollow, even surpassingly cruel, to raped and enslaved Christian women in the Sudan, to beaten and tortured and often killed husbands, to little, battered, sexually abused children, in many Muslim countries. It is the *cross* that proves God's love forever, not our circumstances!

My wife Virginia recently told me about reading the *Voice of the Martyrs* magazine, and about a young man who was arrested and sentenced to life in prison for desecrating the Koran, and he was not even guilty of doing so! They had to keep changing his guards, because he talked to each one of them about Jesus, even though he was in chains! Jesus, with us and in us, and Heaven forever, *that* is the *abundant* life! Sometimes, by the grace of God, our lives may fall in pleasant places, but other times this may not be true.

II Timothy 2:12, declares, *"If we suffer, we shall also reign with him: if we deny him, he also will deny us."* Even more gloriously, II Timothy 3:12 exults, *"Yea, and all that will live godly in Christ Jesus shall suffer persecution."*

Some seem to have misunderstood Paul's burning message in I Timothy 1:8-15:

But we know that the law is good, if a man use it lawfully; Knowing this, that the law is not made for a righteous man, but for the lawless and disobedient, for the ungodly and for sinners, for unholy and profane, for murderers of fathers and murderers of mothers, for manslayers, For whoremongers, for them that defile themselves with mankind, for menstealers, for liars, for perjured persons, and if there be any other thing that is contrary to sound doctrine; According to the glorious gospel of the blessed God, which was committed to my trust. And I thank Christ Jesus our Lord, who hath enabled me, for that he counted me faithful, putting me into the ministry; Who was before a blasphemer, and a persecutor, and injurious: but I obtained mercy, because I did it ignorantly in unbelief. And the grace of our Lord was exceeding abundant with faith and love which is in Christ Jesus. This is a faithful saying, and worthy of all acceptation, that Christ Jesus came into the world to save sinners; of whom I am chief.

Paul is declaring his deliverance from sin here, not declaring his sinfulness! This ignominious list of sins the law exposes, and Paul lists his own particular sins of blaspheming God/Jesus, persecuting, torturing and killing believers, but he no longer does that, because of the grace of God in Christ Jesus, which he received when he was converted on the Damascus road.

Chapter Four – What Does The Holy Spirit Use To Bring Men To Christ?

When he speaks of Christ Jesus coming into this world to save sinners, "of whom I am chief" (present tense), some use this, and perhaps Romans 7, to imply that Paul is still practicing sin, like so many "Christians" of today.

First, Paul is simply stating that he was *the* notorious hater of Jesus and persecutor of Christians, though now saved. I can imagine someone pointing to Paul in his travels, and saying, "Is that the murderous killer of Christians?"

"Yes."

"I understand he has been converted to Christ, and doesn't kill Christians anymore. Is that true?"

"Yes, praise God, it is true!"

The answer may be just that simple.

Second, it was Paul himself, under the inspiration of the Holy Spirit, who triumphantly wrote:

*What shall we say then? Shall we continue in sin, that grace may abound? God forbid. How shall we, that are dead to sin, live any longer therein? Likewise reckon ye also yourselves to be dead indeed unto sin, but alive unto God through Jesus Christ our Lord. Let not sin therefore reign in your mortal body, that ye should obey it in the lusts thereof. Neither yield ye your members as instruments of unrighteousness unto sin: but yield yourselves unto God, as those that are alive from the dead, and your members as instruments of righteousness unto God. For sin shall **not** have dominion over you: for ye are not under the law, but under grace* (Romans 6:1-2, 11-14, emphasis added).

It was Paul, also, who wrote these powerful words:

For they that are after the flesh do mind the things of the flesh; but they that are after the Spirit the things of the Spirit. For to be carnally minded is death; but to be spiritually minded is life and peace. Because the carnal mind is enmity against God: for it is not subject to the law of God, neither indeed can be. So then they that are in the flesh cannot please God. But ye are not in the flesh, but in the Spirit, if so be that the Spirit of God dwell in you. Now if any man have not the Spirit of Christ, he is none of His (Romans 8:5-7).

Vines Expository Dictionary of Old and New Testament Words defines carnal thusly: "1. Sarkikos, from sarx, 'flesh' signifies (a) 'having the nature of flesh,' sensual, controlled by animal appetites, governed by human nature, instead of by the Spirit of God." (pp. 89-90).

Flesh and carnal are used interchangeably. Irrefragably, Paul is declaring that no true Christian can be permanently carnal or live after the flesh. Then he says, "So then they that are in the flesh cannot please God. But ye are *not* in the flesh, but in the Spirit, if so be that the Spirit of God dwell in you. Now if any man have **not** the Spirit of Christ, he is **none** of his" (Romans 8:8-9, emphasis added). (Not a Christian. Christians are not dominated by carnality, they do not live after the flesh). The appellation, carnal Christian, is a misnomer, if used to imply that Christians can live after the flesh and continue to live in sin.

Chapter Four – What Does The Holy Spirit Use To Bring Men To Christ?

Yes, I am aware of I Corinthians 3:1-4, "And I, brethren, could not speak unto you as unto spiritual, but as unto carnal, even as babes in Christ. I have fed you with milk, and not with meat: for hitherto ye were not able to bear it, neither yet now are ye able. For ye are yet carnal: for whereas there is among you envying, and strife, and divisions, are ye not carnal, and walk as men? For while one saith, I am of Paul; and another Apollos, are ye not carnal?"

These relatively new converts from a pagan world of false gods, religious prostitution, gluttony, drunkenness, orgies, and indescribable debauchery, had not yet fully shaken off the shackles of their servitude to the flesh, the world, and the Devil, in some areas of their lives. Nevertheless, as Vine adds, "The Corinthians were making no progress, but they were not anti-spiritual in respect of the particular point with which the apostle was dealing." Vine also claims that the Greek word which should have been translated here, is a kindred, but lest severe word, Sarkinos.

These Corinthian Christians were acting like babes and unregenerate, unsaved men, mainly in one area of their lives, division over the Apostle they preferred! Including the text from chapter one, we find that there were four groups formed, "Christ, Peter, Paul, and Apollos."

As Ernest C. Reisinger, of Founders Ministries, said, "This was a specific outbreak of carnality affecting primarily one area of their lives. And we add, this was *not* the total domination of their lives by the flesh, or carnality."

Let me reiterate Paul's message, "Know ye not that the unrighteous shall not inherit the kingdom of God? Be not deceived: neither fornicators, nor idolaters, nor adulterers, nor effeminate, nor abusers of themselves with mankind, nor thieves, nor covetous, nor drunkards, nor revilers, nor extortioners, shall inherit the kingdom of God. And such *were* some of you, but ye are washed, but ye are sanctified, but ye are justified in the name of the Lord Jesus, and by the Spirit of our God" (I Corinthians 6:9-11, emphasis added).

Look at what they had been delivered from. They were not by today's definition "carnal Christians." For the most part, their lives had been transformed by Christ, or the above verse would make no sense. True, some among them were confused about spiritual gifts, one man was in gross immorality with his father's wife and God caused some among them to be sick or die, because of getting drunk at the Lord's Supper, or love feast.

All of us as Christians are guilty of, or susceptible to, some carnal act or reaction, unless we stay in close and loving fellowship constantly with the Lord Jesus Christ. Our actions can be devastating to our loved ones and us and to our testimony for the Lord Jesus Christ. Truly, a little leaven does leaven the whole lump. Perhaps Ecclesiastes 10:1, sums it up best, "Dead flies cause the ointment of the apothecary to send forth a stinking savour: so doth a little folly him that is in reputation for wisdom and honour."

Remember that it is this same Paul, under the inspiration of the Holy Spirit, who wrote to this same church, "Therefore

Chapter Four – What Does The Holy Spirit Use To Bring Men To Christ?

if any man be in Christ, he is a new creature; old things are passed away; behold, all things are become new" (II Corinthians 5:17).

Many commentators and expositors of the Word of God seem to make one mistake. The ones I have read and the ones I know and have had fellowship with, say something like this, "Brother Mac, you need to realize that this epistle was written to the church. Therefore, you have to interpret everything in it by that standard. It is not written to sinners, or to the lost."

Basically, I agree with this teaching, up to a point. But, God *does* speak to the unsaved in his messages to the churches! He knew that there would be a mixed multitude in the church. He gave warnings in many of the epistles, and other parts of the Bible, that can *only* be applied to the lost. He wants them awakened and saved. He loves them, and must warn them of their real state, professing Christians or not. Romans was written to a church, with a number of passages in it that can only apply to sinners, the lost. "For whosoever shall call upon the name of the Lord shall be saved" (Romans 10:13).

I Corinthians 15:1-4, gives a clear exposition of the Gospel. It identifies what the Gospel is, and calls sinners to salvation, even though this is an epistle to a church! Also, notice Acts 16:31, ". . . Believe on the Lord Jesus Christ, and thou shalt be saved. . ."

Many times, severe warnings are given to the church, not only to wake them up, but also to admonish and draw the lost among them to real salvation. Paul, writing to the churches of the Galatians, called some of them who were demanding faith in Christ, plus circumcision and keeping the law for salvation, "false brethren" (see Galatians 2:4).

After some searing denunciations and warnings to the Galatians, particularly, directed not only to the church, but to the legalists among them, Paul declared, "I desire to be present with you now, and to change my voice; for I stand in doubt of you" (Galatians 4:20).

One of the things Paul was writing to the Corinthians is that they were acting like babes in Christ, even like the unregenerate (see I Corinthians 3:1). His message was, Stop those divisions, which are deadly and carnal. And just in case some did not get the message, the second epistle tells them to "Examine yourselves, whether ye be in the faith; prove your own selves. Know ye not your own selves, how that Jesus Christ be in you, except ye be reprobate" (II Corinthians 13:5).

Is there any epistle to sinners? As such, no! God speaks to sinners through His epistles to the churches, and through the Christians.

Some of the legalistic "Christian" Jews in the book of Hebrews had gone back, or were considering going back, to the Old Testament laws, rituals, and sacrifices. God warned them, in no uncertain terms, that such a move was fatal, and shows vividly the superiority of Christ, and His one sacrifice, paying for sins forever, compared to the insufficient sacrifices of the priests, which were only to point to the one sacrifice, all-sufficient, of Jesus Christ on the cross.

Chapter Four – What Does The Holy Spirit Use To Bring Men To Christ?

After a blistering attack on their condition in Hebrews 6, and a warning that must have jarred them immensely in verses 3-6, Paul alleviates this warning somewhat by saying, "But beloved, we are persuaded better things of you, and things that accompany salvation, though we speak thus" (Hebrews 6:9). This would encourage the true Christians, because they would know that these things did accompany their salvation, and immediately convict the legalists and lost, because these things did not accompany their (supposed) salvation! God's true grace delivers us *from* our sinning. Grace is not a cover for us to keep on sinning.

It is so encouraging to the struggling saint, who has often failed, but loves Jesus, that God loves sinners, but that He also loves His struggling saints. He loves failures! Look at Peter! He loves us, even though we have failed. He longs to envelop us to Himself, and smother us with His forgiving love when we flee to Him and admit we have sinned, and repent of it. I John 1:7b is written primarily to *saints*, ". . . And the blood of Jesus Christ, his Son cleanseth us from all sin." Verse 9 adds the stipulation that those sins must be confessed.

It is a totally different story for someone who has made a decision for Christ and keeps on going his own way, believing that he is eternally secure; believing that grace covers all his sins and therefore he can keep on sinning and still go to Heaven. Better look at I John 3:1-10 very, very carefully! Your eternity may depend on it! If Christians are not witnessing, it is certainly a serious sin.

As an introduction, we will use I John 2:4, "He that saith I know him, and keepeth not his commandments, is a liar, and the truth is not in him." Then God speaks in I John 3:1-10:

Behold, what manner of love the Father hath bestowed upon us, that we should be called the sons of God: therefore the world knoweth us not, because it knew him not. Beloved, now are we the sons of God, and it doth not yet appear what we shall be: but we know that, when he shall appear, we shall be like him; for we shall see him as he is. And every man that hath this hope in him purifieth himself, even as he is pure. Whosoever committeth sin transgresseth also the law: for sin is the transgression of the law. And ye know that he was manifested to take away our sins; and in him is no sin. Whosoever abideth in him sinneth not: whosoever sinneth hath not seen him, neither known him. Little children, let no man deceive you: he that doeth righteousness is righteous, even as he is righteous. He that committeth sin is of the devil; for the devil sinneth from the beginning. For this purpose the Son of God was manifested, that he might destroy the works of the devil. Whosoever is born of God doth not commit [Greek: habitually practice] sin; for his seed remaineth in him: and he cannot sin, because he is born of God. In this the children of God are manifest, and the children of the devil: whosoever doeth not righteousness is not of God neither he that loveth not his brother.

Chapter Four – What Does The Holy Spirit Use To Bring Men To Christ?

For the true Christian, sin, unconfessed and unforsaken, <u>does</u> break fellowship with God. Nothing in this world or the next can break sonship! (See Romans 8:32-39.) However, the true Christian will be miserable and ashamed, and cannot long remain without the fellowship of the God he loves, due to personal sin! Or, if he persists, God may deal with him as He dealt with the sinning Christians at the Lord's Supper (Communion, to some). (See I Corinthians 11:21-34). There is eternal security for the true Christian, or John 3:36a makes no sense, "He that believeth on the Son hath [has, right now] everlasting life." (Also see Hebrews 10:10-14 and I John 5:13.)

In that munificent love of the risen Christ, Paul says, "I say the truth in Christ, I lie not, my conscience also bearing me witness in the Holy Ghost, That I have great heaviness and continual sorrow in my heart. For I could wish that myself were accursed from Christ, for my brethren, my kinsmen according to the flesh" (Romans 9:1-3).

My dearly beloved fellow Christians, do you *know* what Paul just said? Do you grasp the impact of his throbbing heart? He is saying that he would be willing to go to Hell forever if it would result in the salvation of his lost Jewish brethren! He would be willing to give up His much loved Jesus, who is more than life to him. Beatings, torture, prisons, that is nothing to him, if he can win both Jews and Gentiles to Christ. That little poem I learned when I was first saved could not be said of many of us, but certainly of him, "Only one life, 'twill soon be past. Only what's done for Christ will last!"

The Late Great American Church

Chapter Five – The True State of the Unsaved

The True State of the Unsaved

He that believeth on the Son hath everlasting life: and he that believeth not the Son shall not see life; but the wrath of God abideth on him (John 3:36).

Just recently on the TV, I heard a statement from one of the outstanding pastors in America. I cannot help but love and admire him, and he has built a tremendous church; however, this is approximately what he said, "God is Love. He loves everyone. He loves the Muslim and the Mormon, the Baptist and the Methodist, the pagan and the atheist. There is no one that God does not love, because God is love!"

To his credit, he also said, when pressed by an aggressive questioner about whether he believed Christ was the only way to heaven, "I am not the authority on that, but Jesus is, and He said that He is the truth." He was clearly alluding to John 14:6, in which Jesus declared that He was the way, the truth and the life, and that no one could come to the Father except through Him.

It is true that God is love, but equally true that He is Holy, and absolutely cannot stand sin. As he declared through Peter, He is not willing that *any* should perish, PTL (Praise the Lord)!

Years ago, in my evangelistic meetings during the '60s youth movement, so heralded by some as a mighty revival, I held my second set of meetings in Homer, Alaska. I had already been there once, with a powerful movement of God in the church and in the community, where many were saved. This time, probably 15 or 20 young people came in voluntarily to help with the meetings. They spent a good part of their day going out and telling people that God loved them. They were very enthusiastic and effusive about their love for Jesus. No problem with that. I loved it. However, I heard of no conversions through their efforts, as least none they mentioned, or none that came as converts to the church. That was puzzling.

On about the last night of the meetings, three of the leaders of this youth group came forward and wanted to talk with me. Under deep Holy Spirit conviction, all three admitted to me that they did not even know whether they were saved or not, and with broken hearts, pled to be saved.

I led them to Jesus, and noticed a new depth and intensity to their real love for Jesus, and appreciation for His salvation. Part of that was probably because the Holy Spirit almost always caused me to preach on sin, on judgment, and Hell, as well as on the love of Jesus.

One of the key verses that woke me up and haunted me when people ran around telling lost sinners, before they were convicted of sin, that God loved them, was John 3:36. It seemed to me, then and now, that we are giving unrepentant sinners the idea that God's love is wrapped about them like a

Chapter Five – The True State Of The Unsaved

warm blanket, when the *opposite* is true! This false comfort and false assurance may have sent thousands to Hell!

"He that believeth on the Son hath everlasting life: and he that believeth not the Son shall not have life; but the wrath of God abideth on him" (John 3:36). God does not say that the love of God abides on the sinner, but that the *wrath of God abideth* on him!

In Romans, God declares the real picture of the sinner and his imminent danger, "But after thy hardness and impenitent heart treasureth up unto thyself wrath against the day of wrath and revelation of the righteous judgment of God. . ." (2:5). God says every day that passes, the sinner is under the wrath of God, and daily adds to that wrath against the day of wrath when God's mammoth judgment is unleashed on him.

It is true, as noted before, that God commended His love toward us, in that while we were yet sinners, Christ died for us! Marvelous, heart-melting, momentous love! But to know that and not respond to that love is to ignite the fury God already feels towards the breakers of His Holy Law, the contempt for His Son's bloody sacrifice, and the presumption on His grace.

It was in spite of His anger toward the sinner, which sent His beloved Son to the cross, that God so loved the world that He gave His only begotten Son for us, which makes His love even more incredible! God shares the common grace of His love on all men, saved or lost. It rains on one as well as the other. He gives every breath that each man takes, monitors each heartbeat, provides food, and strength to get it, for every person. The goodness of God is meant to lead us to repentance.

Bottom line: "God judgeth the righteous, and God is *angry* with the wicked every day" (Psalm 7:11, emphasis added). God equates every sinner with being wicked, no matter how good or religious the sinner thinks himself to be.

People who are trying to get others to feel good about themselves, and use God's love as a panacea for their problems, need to remember that grace is not a quid pro quo deal. We have *no* worth before God that ensures His grace; the very opposite is true. As Martin Luther said, "God does not love us because we have worth; we have worth because God loves us." But, even that is conditioned by our response to the cross of the Lord Jesus Christ.

God gives a stentorian blast at the wickedness of man in the first three chapters of Romans before He unveils His amazing grace to a lost human race, in Romans 4 through 10.

Lest I be misunderstood, I believe God wants us to be kind and tender to every lost sinner. My wife and I have had multitudes of them in our home, fed them, loved them, helped them with their problems, but always remembered that they were condemned, lost souls, needing first to realize their lost condition, and then to be flooded with God's gracious love to draw them to Christ. I personally believe that one of the reasons God wants us to bear the fruit of the Holy Spirit— Love, Joy, Peace, Longsuffering, Gentleness, Goodness, Faith, Meekness, and Temperance—is to display Christ to others, to represent Christ to the lost.

Chapter Five – The True State Of The Unsaved

One reason to be good to the lost sinner is that this world, with its doleful dirge of tragedies, heartbreak and death, is their *heaven*! This is the best it will ever be for them, unless they come to know the Lord Jesus Christ. A far greater reason is to love them with the love Jesus has for them, even as He warned them of their condemnation, and even wept over them, as He did over Jerusalem. Perhaps <u>you</u> will be able to lead them to Christ.

If God did not love them, His wrath, which now abides on them, His anger, which is with them every day, would soon reach flash point, and explode them into an eternal Hell without delay. By offending His love, and going their own way, sinners put themselves squarely under His smoldering wrath, building up against them every day like some huge avalanche. Any moment, night or day, the last snowflake may fall that triggers this colossus of doom to thunder down upon them. His Holiness can hardly tolerate another sin, another broken law, while the sinner goes blithely on his way.

Speaking of those who have gone away from Him, God says, ". . . Yea, they have chosen their own ways, and their soul delighteth in their abomination. I will also choose their delusions, and will bring their fears upon them; because when I called, none did answer; when I spake they did not hear: but they did evil before mine eyes, and chose that in which I delighted not" (Isaiah 66:3b-4).

Hundreds of thousands of individuals raised in Christian homes, taken to solid evangelical churches, where they heard the truth, rebelled, and then later became avid members of some cult, or some form of unbelief. Most of them will never be delivered. Because of their contempt for their church, their parents, and especially the Gospel of the Lord Jesus Christ, they rebelled and went their own way. God chose their delusion. It is enough to make the angels weep, as well as some Christians.

In seeking to discover why about 98 percent of today's Christians never become soul-winners, I listed some factors, and there are others. One factor is the common idea I hear from many pulpits.

First, I want to distinguish between "witnessing" and "soul-winning." I have never known a man to willing go fishing day after day, week after week, and never catch a fish. I have never seen a man who did a lot of fishing, and really wanted to catch fish, shrug his shoulders and say, "Well, it doesn't matter whether I catch any fish or not, I just like to go fishing." That might be true for a few unproductive trips, but for hundreds of trips in a lifetime?

I have never known a farmer who planted his crop, watered his crop, fertilized and cultivated his crop, and then let it rot in the field! God gave the crop life, man cannot do that, but man *can* reap it. God does not reap the crop for the farmer. The farmer must reap his own crop.

The same is true of reaping sinners.

So often I hear, "You just be faithful. Sow the seed, tell them about Jesus, and pray for them. That is your responsibility. Leave the rest up to God. He is the one who wins souls, not you!"

Chapter Five – The True State Of The Unsaved

That sounds very pious, trusting, and spiritual, does it not? It gives God all the glory! In reality, though, it is often a cop-out, and a cover for unbelief. Not always, but often.

Let me repeat something said earlier. Peter and his buddies, James and John, had fished all night and caught nothing. Jesus directed them to throw out their nets for fish. Peter gave a classic and honest answer. "And Simon answering said unto him, Master, we have toiled all the night, and have taken nothing. Nevertheless, at thy word I will let down the net" (Luke 5:5).

Bone-weary, tired, sleepy, dirty, hungry Peter did NOT feel like going fishing! It meant that he would have to clean his net again (no little chore) when he had already cleaned it. Besides, he obviously thought it was a useless effort, an exercise in futility. Yet by faith, at the command of the Jesus he loved, he let down the net, and to his astonishment got a net full of fish.

Notice several things, (1) Jesus was illustrating vividly that He could direct them miraculously in catching fish, (2) He was not satisfied with them just fishing and not catching any fish, any more than they were, (3) He knew right where the fish were, (4) He did not catch them Himself, but caught them through the disciples, and (5) Jesus intended it as a graphic, dramatic picture they could never forget concerning soul-winning.

Jesus drove the point home like a lance to the heart, "And so was also James, and John, the sons of Zebedee, which were partners with Simon. And Jesus said unto Simon, fear not; from henceforth thou *shalt* catch men" (Luke 5:10, emphasis added).

Fishing is witnessing. You will never catch any fish in your bathtub. You must leave your comfort zone and go fishing, or you will never catch any fish. Soul-winning! Now *that* is when you catch the fish you are fishing for!

We are commissioned not just to fish, but to *catch*. In the Great Commission, Jesus sums it up neatly:

And Jesus came and spake unto them, saying, *"All power is given unto me in heaven and in earth. Go ye therefore, and teach all nations, baptizing them in the name of the Father, and of the Son, and of the Holy Ghost: Teaching them to observe all things whatsoever I have commanded you; and lo, I am with you always, even unto the end of the world. Amen"* (Matthew 28:18-20).

Vine adds that this word, teaching (Greek: Matheteuo) equates with the word "disciple," meaning that Christians are not just to sow the seed, but to actually make disciples, and baptize them, and continue to teach them the Word of God. It is interesting and thrilling to see that Jesus said all power is given unto Him; and then, "Go ye therefore," signifying that it was His power through us that was going to do the mighty work. It is worth noting that He said, "Lo, I am with you always," apparently just to those who involve themselves in obeying the Great Commission, or at the very least, considering the context, most especially with them.

Chapter Five – The True State Of The Unsaved

"The fruit of the righteous is a tree of life; and he that winneth souls is wise" (Proverbs 11:30).

Not just shares Jesus, or witnesses, wonderful as that is, but wins souls. "The harvest truly is plenteous, but the labourers are few; Pray ye therefore the Lord of the harvest, that he will send forth labourers into harvest" (Matthew 9:37b-38). What were the labourers to do? Sow some more seed? Share the good news? Yes, but *more*, they were to *reap* the harvest!

So we are to *catch*, to *make disciples, reap,* and *win souls*. That is our commission, not just to witness, which is the means to an end, the salvation of souls!

Finally, Psalms embodies a major promise, "He that goeth forth and weepeth, bearing precious seed, shall doubtless come again with rejoicing, bringing his sheaves with him" (126:6). The ineluctable truth enunciated here is that those who go forth with weeping, a real passion for the lost souls of men, bearing the word of God, which is shared with these sinners, will absolutely without fail come again with rejoicing, bringing the sheaves, the harvest, lost souls that God has used him to win to Christ.

I do *not* leave it up to God to reap the harvest. God leaves it up to me! He furnishes the power and the passion, but I do it. He gets *all* the glory. I am involved in the winning of souls; it is my heart that is broken in concert with His. John 15 tells us that "without Him we can do nothing," but if we are Christians we are not without Him, unless we try to do what we do for Him in the flesh, for our own honor and glory. But Philippians 4:13 triumphantly shouts, "I can do all things through Christ who strengtheneth me." That certainly includes soul-winning, God's first priority.

Jesus wept over Jerusalem. Paul wept over those he warned. We need to be involved with all we are, heart, mind and will, in pursuing souls for Christ. His passion will begin to flow through us as we go consistently out to share Christ and seek to win souls to Christ.

I do not just teach witnessing classes. I teach soul-winning classes. That subtle distinction has made a world of difference. Because some are so afraid they will put a guilt trip on Christians who have never won a soul, even though they may witness, they comfort them in their unbelief that God will win souls through them, or that it is even their responsibility. We, even as Christians, still have the Old Sin Nature. If we can find an easy way out, it is all too tempting to take it, especially when we are made to believe we have done our duty if we just "witness."

No, I am not denigrating witnessing. It is fantastic and wonderful when an individual, a church, or a group of Christians seriously begins to witness, to share Christ. Even if they just shared, and prayed, and waited on the Lord, sooner or later some would come to Christ, but nothing like the harvest God wants. We have not believed Him and His promises, and done what He told us to do. Win souls.

Chapter Five – The True State Of The Unsaved

How many fishermen have you ever known who could keep excited about fishing and keep going year after year, if they never caught any fish?

What happens is that many begin witnessing after some powerful stimulation from an evangelist or pastor, or from their own heart conviction. With few if any souls coming to Christ, they begin to drop out, and the soul-winning program of the church, and their own lives, is shot! It is disillusioning and discouraging, so the leader may tell them, "Just keep on witnessing and don't worry about the results. God will take care of that." A few may drift back.

God *will* take care of winning souls, but He does it through *us*. That is not my choice; it is His. You *can* win souls, dear Christian. God said so. Please do not let the one or two, or hundreds or thousands, you might have won to Christ, go to Hell.

If you had kept on, by faith believed God's promise, and sought to win them to Christ, sooner or later some precious soul would have been born again, and you would have tasted the elixir of life! Life can become almost unbearably exciting when you see Jesus work through you, to save some precious lost soul. You will enjoy them here on earth, and spend eternity with them in Heaven! Expect God to win souls through you to His eternal glory, for their salvation from the Lake of Fire. He will, if you never quit.

Sometimes, when I am sitting in Church, I see what seem to be the sweetest, godliest, most precious saints I have ever known. I have been in hundreds of churches, and I am in a fine church now, as a member. I have found saints who pray more than I do. I have found saints who seem to have grown in Christ more than I have. I have seen saints who work around the church much more than I do, performing all kinds of hard, menial tasks to the glory of the Lord. I thought that at least I was doing a fair job of reading my Bible, thinking that at a guess I had read it through 20-25 times, until I met a lady in Alaska who was 75 years old and had read it through 75 times. I had about recovered from that shock, when I discovered that Dr. Robert Summer, who edits the *Biblical Evangelist*, has read his Bible through 180 times. Are these things not glorifying to God? Do they not count? Of course they do, not to be saved or stay saved, but to demonstrate a deep love for the Lord Jesus Christ.

Could it be beloved friends, Bible scholars, multitude of Christians and professing Christians, that I am wrong? Could it be that I have fallen into the trap that because something appeals to me, and my spiritual gift seems to center on soul-winning, that I am being harsh on many dear and beloved true Christians and pastors? Suppose my gift was giving, and I loved to give, and became like one famous Christian who gave nine-tenths of all he earned to the Lord, and tithed the other tenth? Suppose then I looked with disdain upon all non-givers, or at least on those who barely gave a tenth, and cast aspersions on their Christianity?

I have friends whose gift is Bible teaching, and they study the Word assiduously and with great joy and share the truths they find with enthusiasm and delight, to the honor and glory of God. Suppose they felt that those who did not study the Bible with alacrity and obedience to II Timothy 2:15 as the most important command in the Bible, were perhaps not even Christians, or at the very least, were guilty and suspect before God? ("Study to shew [show] thyself approved unto God, a workman that needeth not to be ashamed, rightly dividing the word of truth.")

Suppose my passion was prayer, or showing mercy, or caring for the poor, or visiting the sick, or encouraging others? Yes, I could be wrong. I almost hope that I am, though it would shatter me to know that I have misled the saints, and misunderstood the Word of God.

It grieves me terribly to consider that millions of Christians are deliberately refusing to share Christ with lost souls. Perhaps we really are soul-murderers, at least potentially, if other things, however godly, can keep us from what Christ came for—to seek and save that which was lost! In fact, many of the gifts and passions of those I listed above actually lend themselves to soul-winning, and open the door to that joy, but thousands are doing these other things, ostensibly to the glory of God, and yet not winning souls, or at least not getting serious about their witness.

Deep in my heart, a tiny but insistent little voice reminds me, *But they and you can do all this and still miss the best.* Do you realize now that all these good things can be a balm to cover the conscience of those who refuse or neglect to warn the lost? Hopefully, this service and worship is obedience and love for the Lord Jesus Christ, but if it is, it should lead to the one thing Christ died for, the souls of men He sends us to reach!

I hear so many times that we are saved to be conformed to the image of Christ. True. "Now the Lord is that Spirit: and where the Spirit of the Lord is, there is liberty. But we all, with open face beholding as in a glass the glory of the Lord, are changed into the same image from glory to glory, even as by the Spirit of the Lord" (II Corinthians 3:17-18).

A dear friend of mine, Fred Dyson (I introduced him to his wife to be, Jane), came excitedly over to my house one day about 35 years ago, and expounded that verse to me. It has had a new dimension for me ever since.

As I constantly contemplate Jesus and His glory and His love, and His sacrifice for me, and look at Him in His word, the Bible, I become like Him, conformed to His image, more and more, by the Spirit of the Lord. That is true of any and all of us. But it is impossible to be conformed to His image and not love souls. He came to seek and save the lost, and if I am conformed to His image, His love and His desire will become my love, my desire!

Some seem to think that being conformed to His image is what it is all about. The implication sometimes seems to be that it is far more important than soul-winning. You cannot possibly be conformed to the image of Christ, to the image of one who said, "For the Son of man is come to seek and to save that which was lost" (Luke 19:10) and not be a soul-winner, and not have a passion for souls. He did, and it consumed Him.

Chapter Five - The True State Of The Unsaved

Jesus is the bridegroom, and He is preparing us, the church, as His forever bride. Do you think He wants a bride with the blood of lost sinners on her hands?

Of course, being forgiving; bearing the fruit of the Holy Spirit; loving God with all our heart, mind and soul, and our neighbor as ourselves; forsaking sin in thought, word and deed; speaking the truth in love; loving and sharing with the poor and downtrodden; feeding the hungry; praising and worshipping the Lord; being kind and sensitive to others; feeding on the Word of God; and having constant sweet fellowship with Jesus, is all part of being conformed to His image.

Yet if we did all of these things, and let souls go to Hell without warning them, this could invalidate all else mentioned, except that, if all this was <u>really</u> true of our relationship with Jesus, we would seek the lost. It is *impossible* to truly love Jesus, and not love the lost.

Anything else may give us warm titillations, but is a delusion of Satan, or at least of our own flesh. Do not hide behind your good works, or spiritual growth, or supposed love and worship of Jesus, or good feelings when you praise Him, and let souls go to the Lake of Fire.

Pastors, teachers, and congregations in most churches I have visited seem more concerned that no one rocks the boat, that we love one another (vitally important and one of the signs of a true Christian), that we love and praise the Lord together, that we really study the Bible and pray, and that each one does his part and uses his gifts in the body of Christ. It is also nice if someone comes to Christ now and then, as a sort of "icing on the cake."

Such an attitude would apply to almost any average church or any average body of Christians in the country, but is *fatal* to the cause of Christ. It sets up a comfort zone of introspective narcissism, while any burning passion to reach souls for Christ seems oddball and counter-productive to the real purpose of the church, as such congregations see it. Love Jesus, be happy, love one another, and take no risks. Rock-a-bye, baby!

As we mentioned before, but need to stress again, some pastors and evangelists seem inordinately afraid of offending people. To be strident, negative, and contentious to the point of driving someone away from Jesus and His salvation is an abomination to God. It violates His love. His warnings against offending are thunderous. Yet Jesus, tender, gentle, and loving, the master soul-winner of all time, offended so many so powerfully and directly that He was crucified in bloody agony. The Gospel *will* offend, at times, if not accepted.

Some of these same pastors have offended many who have left their churches, yet suppress any real, bold, heartbreaking soul-winning by squelching those who are soul-winners or potential soul-winners. I have been in churches where the pastor, though he asked me to hold evangelistic meetings, did not want me to go out knocking on doors, because it might embarrass him or someone in the church!

Chapter Five – The True State Of The Unsaved

Never offend deliberately, always apologize when you do, in the tender love of Christ, but let no timid pastor, who usually takes the side of the sinner against you if the sinner says you offended him, dull your passion for souls. I would a million times rather offend someone, though I weep when I do, than offend a Holy God and not witness! I have attended churches where "offending" someone by witnessing to them was treated almost like the unpardonable sin, and made the Christian, who deep in his heart wanted to reach the lost, shrink back because he did not know if he would do it right. That type of church is usually devoid of soul-winners, or even witnessing "Christians," thereby letting lost men and women go to Hell, and that is by far the greatest offense against lost souls and a Holy God.

Could such pastors and churches really believe in Hell? That offense is dooming millions that will never hear of the wonderful love and grace of our Lord Jesus Christ. Dear pastors of such churches, do you know what you are doing? You are doing Satan's work for him while serving Christ, you believe, with all your heart. I love you, but God help you.

Nevertheless, thousands of godly pastors are some of the greatest soul-winners and trainers of soul-winners in the world today! Praise the Lord for them!

Anyone who deliberately causes division or trouble in the church is an abomination to God. He is anathema to the Church. Look closely at Romans 16:17, "Now I beseech you, brethren, mark them which cause divisions and offences *contrary to the doctrine which ye have learned*, and avoid them" (emphasis added). The doctrine we have learned, from the Word of God and from the Lord Jesus Christ, is to seek souls for Him, for their salvation and for His glory. It is those who are not seeking souls and who are causing division in the Church who are acting contrary to this doctrine. "As my father hath sent me, even so send I you" (John 20:21b).

"And he said unto them, Go ye into all the world, and preach the gospel to every creature" (Mark 16:15). We can let nothing, not even good things, deter us from the main purpose of God.

Ray Comfort nails it down pretty well:

There was once a respectable captain of a ship, whose crew spoke highly of him. They said they esteemed him to a point where everyone knew of their professed love for him.

One day, however, the captain saw, to his horror, that an ocean liner had struck an iceberg and people were drowning in the freezing water ahead of his ship. He quickly directed his vessel to the area, stood on the bridge, and made an impassioned plea to his crew to throw out the life preservers. Instead of obeying his charge, the crew lifted up their hands and said, "Praise the captain . . . praise you . . . we love you! You are worthy of our praise."

Can you see that the reality of their adoration *should have been manifest by their obedience to his command?* Their "admiration" was nothing but empty words (*Revival's Golden Key,* 2002, pp. 179-180).

Chapter Five – The True State Of The Unsaved

So it is with us, if we do not obey Christ in reaching the lost. All the praise, worship, and professed love in such a case is religious froth!

The Christian Holocaust

They on the rock are they, which, when they hear, receive the word with joy; and these have no root, which for a while believe, and in time of temptation fall away (Luke 8:13).

As Jesus wept over Jerusalem, may we weep with Him over America today. The following is why an urgent, powerful, Spirit-filled, yet loving, gentle, broken-hearted witness, in the Love of Christ, is needed from every true Christian. Read it and weep. And pray. And witness.

Author/Evangelist Ray Comfort has come to believe that the parable of the sower given in Matthew 13, Mark 4, and Luke 8, is the God-given key to opening up other parables. For instance, in explaining to the puzzled disciples the meaning of the parable of the sower, Jesus said, "And he said unto them, Know ye not this parable? And how then will ye know all parables?" (Mark 4:13).

The sower parable explicitly teaches the difference between the false and true convert; only one out of four went on with the Lord. Comfort then applies the same principle to the Wise and Foolish Virgins, the Wheat and Tares, the Good and Bad Fish, the Goats and Sheep, and the Wise and Foolish House Builders. All deal with the false and the true, a problem that has reached epidemic proportions in today's "Christians" and the churches in our beloved America.

It is in this parable, in one segment as given in Luke, that we learn that there is a false belief, which does not save. "They on the rock are they which, when they hear, receive the word with joy; and these have no root, which for a while believe, and in time of temptation fall away" (Luke 8:13).

I John 2:19 explains why they were never saved; they were "not all of us," not true Christians from the beginning. God says, "They went out from us, but they were not all of us; for if they had been of us, they would no doubt have continued with us; but they went out, that they might be made manifest that they were not all of us."

Sometimes my beloved wife Virginia puts me on the spot. She says, "Mac, are you saying that only soul-winners are saved? That is what it sounds like." She is a soul-winner, but she bristles at that idea. It seems to shred grace.

The answer is, "No, not exactly." But let's take another look at God's definition of grace.

"For the grace of God that bringeth salvation hath appeared to all men, Teaching us that, denying ungodliness and worldly lusts, we should live soberly, righteously, and godly, in this present world, Looking for that blessed hope, and the glorious appearing of the great God, and our Saviour Jesus Christ; Who gave himself for us, that he might redeem us from all iniquity, and purify unto himself a peculiar people, zealous of good works" (Titus 2:11-14).

Chapter Six - The Christian Holocaust

This verse kills the "turning the grace of our God into lasciviousness, and denying the only Lord God, and our Lord Jesus Christ," mentioned in Jude 4. It slaughters antinomianism (lawlessness: since all our sins are forgiven, past, present and future, and we are not under the law, we can live in sin, go our own way, and rejoice in our freedom in Christ). A fatal delusion!

Here is the glorious freedom in Christ that Christians have, *not* the freedom to continue to sin and go our own way! "Looking for that blessed hope and the glorious appearing of the great God and our Saviour, Jesus Christ." (One will appear, Jesus Christ, who is God, as this verse clearly says.)

It tells us why, by His grace, Jesus saved us: to redeem us from all iniquity, and purify unto Himself a peculiar people, *zealous of good works*!

Can anyone who is godly deliberately let sinners go to the Lake of Fire without warning them? If he could, would that not discredit all his other supposed godliness?

Jessica Lang, the precious little girl, nine years old, snatched from her warm bed, her home, by a sex predator, tortured and sexually raped over and over again for days, was allowed to keep her teddy bear. When this sexual predator finally killed her, he buried the teddy bear with her. How touching! He violated her, murdered her, but he let her have her teddy bear. (Actually, he buried her alive.) How many of us are murdering lost souls, but giving God a teddy bear of our devotion and good works?

If a person has no love for, and no desire to reach the lost, at least to witness to and pray for them, he has missed the boat; you have not, if you are faithfully sharing Jesus.

I have used considerable space to answer my dear sweetheart wife, Virginia, when she asked me, "Mac, do you believe only soul-winners are saved?"

It *would* shred grace to say one has to be a soul-winner to be saved! It would destroy Ephesians 2:8-9. It would violate Romans 4:1-5. It would take glory away from the Lord Jesus Christ, who shed His blood to wash away *all* our sins, and needs no help from us to save our souls. He *alone* saves us forever.

"Even so then at this present time also there is a remnant according to the election of grace. And if by grace, then is it no more of works: otherwise grace is no more grace. But if it be of works, then is it no more grace: otherwise work is no more work" (Romans 11:5-6).

This is God's classic answer. The remnant saved in Jeremiah's day, when many others perished, were not saved because of their good works, or because they were better than the other Israelites. They only responded positively to the grace of God. The multitudes did not.

For balance, however, we must not forget James 2:22, "Seest thou how faith wrought with his works, and by works was faith made perfect?" We must not make the mistake some have made and perform such a complete dichotomy between faith and works that works become irrelevant.

Chapter Six – The Christian Holocaust

True faith produces works, as James notes, "But wilt thou know, O vain man, that faith without works is dead?" (2:20).

Here is what I can say, Virginia. God's Word says that, if we follow Jesus, he will make us fishers of men. Luke 5:10b tells us, ". . . from henceforth thou shalt catch men." Luke 19:10 declares, "For the Son of man is come to seek and to save that which was lost." John 20:21b adds, ". . . as my Father hath sent me, even so send I you." Not much theological undulation there, just a cannon shot straight to the heart of any true Christian.

So if a Christian is not a soul-winner, or at least a witness seeking to win souls, he does not have the passion and love of Christ in him to reach the lost. Why? However devoted he may be or seem to be in other areas of the Christian life, he is disobeying God in this most crucial area.

Or he has been badly taught and coddled in his comfort zone to believe that this is not his responsibility. Or there is some sin in his life that he is battling, and he feels like he would be a hypocrite if he witnessed (one of Satan's ploys). Or he intends to witness when he "grows" enough. Or he is afraid he will offend somebody. Or it interferes with his life and his time.

Or he is a backslidden Christian (most of those are lost, in my opinion). Or he is a professing Christian, but he is not saved.

One horrible possibility, but I pray with all my heart that such is not the case, is that the insipid Christianity we have so much of in America is a signal that about 90 percent of our so-called "Christians" are on the "broad" way that leads to Hell.

I John was written that we might *know* that we have eternal life, with assurance given from things believed, and from obedience. There is no place in the Book that says you have to be a soul-winner to know that you are saved. I John 5:13, sums it up. In fact, a man can be a soul-winner and not be saved, if he is depending on that to save or help save him.

Yet I John 2:4 packs a tremendous wallop! "He that saith, I know him, and keepeth not his commandments, is a liar, and the truth is not in him."

In Acts 1:8 we are told that we are His witnesses. In the Great Commission we are told to "go into all the world and preach the gospel to every creature." Certainly, not winning souls fits into the mold of those who keep not his commandments, and therefore are declared to be liars, and devoid of the truth. While it is not for us to judge individuals, in some situations God does tell us to "judge righteous judgment" (John 7: 24).

To be completely honest, Virginia, I would be very concerned about any Christian who had been a Christian any length of time, if he or she, not only was not a soul-winner, but had no interest in sharing their faith, in witnessing. Many wonderful and precious Christian people have been witnesses for Christ, both by life and lips, but have seen few or no souls come to Christ. Praise God for them that they keep at it. Maybe they were not taught, or failed to believe, that they

Chapter Six – The Christian Holocaust

could have had the ineffable joy of winning precious souls to Christ. Yet God guarantees that we can win souls.

Sometimes others may have harvested those they witnessed to, PTL! However, it is very probable that thousands who could have been won to Christ perished and went to Hell because those who witnessed to them did not follow through to win them to Christ.

Let me reiterate. Works do not save, or keep you saved. Jesus alone does. Soul-winning does not save or keep you saved. Jesus does. Works do demonstrate the reality of our salvation. Soul-winning, sharing in Christ's passion for the lost, demonstrates the reality of our salvation.

We cannot demonstrate what we do not have. That is my fear for those who say they are saved and let a lost world around them go to Hell without Christ. I cannot comprehend how anyone with the love of the Lord Jesus Christ in them can let people die and go to the Lake of Fire while they continue to sing, "Oh, How I love Jesus."

Imagine a man with a beautiful home on the beach strolling on the sand in front of his house. He is collecting pretty stones. Suddenly, a stove explodes in his lovely home. The fire is all over his home in a few minutes. His wife and two twin baby daughters are trapped upstairs, and screaming for help. He calls out to them how much he loves them! He continues to pick up stones on the beach, and is suddenly transfixed by one of them, a real beauty. While his house collapses with a roar, he continues to admire the beautiful stone. That, my dear friend, is criminal. How can it be any different with those who ignore the plight of lost souls?

Is what I have said, my dear, sweet Virginia, and my inquisitive reader, a shredding of grace? I do not believe so. I am concerned with anyone and their true salvation, if they have no passion for souls.

One of the greatest writers on grace outside of the Bible, Charles Spurgeon, soul-winner and pastor extraordinaire, agrees with me. He authored the book, *All of Grace*, a blessing to me years ago as a young Christian.

The following quote appears in Ray Comfort's book, *Revivals Golden Key*:

Charles Spurgeon said, "Have you no wish for others to be saved? Then you are not saved yourself. Be sure of that." He continued, "The saving of souls, if a man has once gained love to perishing sinners and his blessed Master, will be an all-absorbing passion to him. It will so carry him away, that he will almost forget himself in the saving of others. He will be like the brave fireman, who cares not for the scorch or the heat, so that he may rescue the poor creature on whom true humanity has set its heart. If sinners will be damned, at least let them leap to Hell over our bodies. And if they will perish, let them perish with our arms about their knees, imploring them to stay. If hell must be filled, at least let it be filled in the teeth of our exertions, and let not one go there unwarned and unprayed for" (pp. 169-170).

Chapter Six – The Christian Holocaust

Some years ago, I read the story of a man who was witnessing to an atheist. The atheist scoffed at him, and said something like this, "You Christians teach that all sinners, all those without Christ, die and go to a terrible place called the Lake of Fire, to burn and scream forever and forever, with no hope. If I truly believed that, I'd crawl on my bare knees, if necessary, over broken glass, day and night, to plead with all I could to become Christians and flee that awful place. Nothing else would matter. Yet I see very few of you Christians seriously making that the priority in your lives. I don't believe you really believe in Hell. How could you and be so cruel, so indifferent, so callous? And if you don't believe it, why do you expect me to?"

Dear beloved, fellow Christians, and churches, especially here in opulent America, I beseech you in the name of the Lord Jesus Christ, please wake up, and join the Lord Jesus Christ in His great love for the lost. We have rabid enemies, inside and outside the church. Time is fleeting; life is uncertain; life is a vapor. Let us put soul-winning absolutely *first* in our lives, and in our churches. Oh dear God, please wake us up, for Jesus' sake and for the sake of lost souls.

To be fair to the many dear pastors and friends I love who say, "You just tell them about Christ, and leave the rest up to God." This is true in some sense, sometimes. I have the CD of a precious man, "The Little White-haired Man," who gave out tracts for many years on a busy street while simultaneously asking people if they were saved, if they knew Jesus and were going to heaven, and got *no* encouragement, and knew of no one who had been saved! Yet he continued faithfully! Makes me want to weep.

Some godly men, some of whom had been saved by this witness and tracts, searched indefatigably, in several nations, until they discovered well over 100,000 people who had become Christians through this little white-haired man. God, true to His Word, did let him know about the sheaves a few days before his death. (See Psalm 126:6.)

I beg of you; I implore you, in the name of the Lord Jesus Christ, *commit* yourself to loving Jesus more than life, and to loving, witnessing, and winning souls to Him. Start now. Commit yourselves, with no turning back! Please get and read *So Send I You*, a companion to this book, for even more explicit instructions.

For starters, as Comfort says, drop the bomb of the law on sinners, that they may see their sinfulness and urgent need of the Lord Jesus Christ.

Here is a simple method that has helped many. Write this list in the front of your Bible:

- Romans 3:23
- Romans 6:23
- Isaiah 53:6
- Ephesians 2:8-9
- John 3:3
- John 1:12
- Romans 10:9-10

Chapter Six - The Christian Holocaust

- Romans 10:13

I simply read, or preferably have the prospect read, these verses aloud. Then I explain very briefly and simply what the verses mean, letting the prospect express what he thinks, and if he understands them.

If he accepts Christ, lead him back to Romans 10:13, and on to John 3:36, and I John 5:13. Let him pray, or lead him in praying, the sinners' prayer. When the Holy Spirit has worked on the Word of God to redeem him through the blood of the Lord Jesus Christ and His sacrifice and resurrection, and when he really believes John 3:36, being careful to explain what saving belief really is, have him thank the Lord Jesus Christ for saving his soul. Then it is good to lead him to John 14:23, and approach him about public confession and baptism, church attendance, reading the Word, praying, and sharing Christ. Make an appointment to follow through in 24 to 48 hours.

To review the approach and presentation again; when beginning with Romans 3:23, go to Exodus 20 and use several of the commandments to let the law convince him of his lost estate before a Holy God.

You can simply write Exodus 20 on the page Romans 3:23 is on, with several simple words to remind you, like, "Do not steal, lie, commit adultery, kill, put no other gods, including yourself, before the one True God of the Bible," etc. It is good to explain that Jesus calls looking on a woman, or man, to lust after them, "adultery." Ask if they have ever done that. Then what, in God's sight, does that make them? (See Matthew 5:28.)

Likewise, God's Word says, "Whosoever hateth his brother is a murderer; and ye know that no murderer hath eternal life abiding in him" (I John 3:15). Ask the person you are dealing with if he has ever hated anyone. Do the same with lying, and share with them that God says liars have their part in the Lake of Fire (see Revelation 21:8), and ask them if they have ever lied. The same may be done with stealing, and with putting anything else before God, including "going their own way and being their own god," a fatal mistake (see Isaiah 53:6).

Jim Tetlow and Ray Comfort have been used by God to do a great job with this approach. Jim Tetlow made a video about using this technique on the streets of New York, called "The Good Test," to shatter the common idea that we are "good" people, and not desperate sinners one heartbeat from Hell.

Write the verses you listed in the front of your Bible this way:

- By Romans 3:23, write Romans 6:23, your next verse.
- By Romans 6:23, write Isaiah 53:6.
- By Isaiah 53:6, write Ephesians 2:8-9.
- By Ephesians 2:8-9, write John 3:3.
- By John 3:3, write John 1:12.

Chapter Six – The Christian Holocaust

- By John 1:12, write Romans 10:9-10.
- By Romans 10:9-10, write Romans 10:13.

When sharing Christ with this method, this should be the time to ask the prospect if they realize they are a lost sinner, needing Jesus. Ask if they know that He was God and died on the cross for their sins, shedding His blood on the cross for them (us). He was separated from God the Father in our place, bearing our sins. Jesus rose bodily from the dead on the third day, and offers salvation to them by faith if they will accept Him and trust in Him with all their heart.

If they are ready, have them call on the Lord Jesus Christ to save them, forgive them. Assure them that according to Romans 10:13, if they understand their need of salvation and call on Him with true faith, He must save them because He promised and cannot lie. Besides, if He loved them enough to die for them, to shed His blood for them on that cross of agony and shame, He would *never* turn them down! When they have called on Jesus for salvation, lead them to assurance by the Word of God, especially using Romans 10:13, John 3:36a, and I John 5:13.

Again, have them pray twice. Lead them in prayer, or let them pray their own salvation prayer, as they desire. Then when it is clear to them by the Holy Spirit using the Word of God, which you will show them, ask them if they KNOW by the Word of God, John 3:36, that they now have everlasting life. When they are sure, using Romans 10:13 and I John

5:13, if necessary, rejoice together in their salvation! Have them thank God, out loud, for saving their soul, forgiving them, and giving them everlasting life.

Then you can talk to them about living for Jesus because He has saved them and loves them. Baptism, prayer, reading the Bible daily, faithful church attendance, and sharing Christ, should be introduced to them—as well as what to do when they sin. Remind them that the Christian life is primarily Christ living His life through them.

God bless you! Get going! As Jesus said in John 20:21b, ". . . So Send I You!"

(If you have the author's book by this title, the 11th chapter gives an excellent method of how to lead people to Jesus Christ.) If you do not like this method, there are plenty of others, or develop your own presentation. Be sure it is accurate Biblically, and go prayerfully in the love of Jesus Christ!

Goodbye "Christian" America: The Desperate Need of Dying Churches

Wherefore do ye spend money for that which is not bread? and your labour for that which satisfieth not? hearken diligently unto me, and eat ye that which is good, and let your soul delight itself in fatness (Isaiah 55:2).

What is the answer to the false decisions, and pitiful condition of the church, and new "converts" today?

The answer to that might require another book, but here it is, in brief. We must get sinners under conviction by the use of the Holy Law of God. (See Exodus 20.) We must mightily show that life is a vapor; the sinner is one heartbeat from Hell, day and night, and urgently needs a Savior!

We must stress the Lordship of Christ. "That if thou shalt confess with thy mouth the Lord Jesus [literally, that *Jesus is Lord*], and shalt believe in thine heart that God hath raised him from the dead, thou shalt be saved" (Romans 10:9).

"And he said to them all, If any man will come after me, let him deny himself, and take up his cross daily, and follow me" (Luke 9:23). Real Christianity produces *followers of Jesus*, not those who continue going their own way (see Isaiah 53:6).

We must show by the Bible how to become children of God. We can reveal the fact that Jesus can help us with any problem, here and now, and solve life's mystery as to where we came from, why we are here, and where we are going. We can show exactly how we can receive His forgiveness by His shed blood. We must stress the glory of Heaven and the compassion of Jesus. We can declare that the wonderful love of Jesus, and abundant life and peace in Him, can be ours now, no matter how dire our circumstances. We must declare with Scripture the horror of Hell, of the Lake of Fire. We must stress often an eternity with no Christ, no God, and no Hope.

We must show who Jesus was, and is, and what He did for us. The Holy Spirit must bring on conviction, and He does it through the Word of God.

We must bring the new convert to an absolute KNOW-SO salvation, by the Word of God, and have him thank God for that salvation after He has prayed to receive Christ. (See Romans 10:13, John 3:36, and especially I John 5:13.)

The new convert must be given verses like John 14:23, which indicates that real love is shown by our obedience, demonstrating our salvation. John 13:35 and I John 3:14 illustrate that point even further. Hebrews 10:25 speaks of the churching of ourselves together. The new convert should be immediately shown the outworking of his becoming a new creature in Christ, as pictured in baptism, church attendance, reading his Bible, prayer, sharing his faith, and loving Jesus and others. He needs to begin developing an intimate personal relationship with the Lord Jesus Christ.

Chapter Seven – Goodbye Christian America: The Desperate Need of Dying Churches

The new convert should be led to I John 1:9 and find out that although no Christian can continue habitually in sin, a Christian, although he now has a new nature and has Christ dwelling in him, still has the old nature and can sin. But he can confess that sin, and receive instant forgiveness, and God will help him to repent and forsake that sin.

The soul-winner should see that the new convert is discipled, either by himself, or by some competent mentor.

Our churches are filled with false Christians, trying desperately to live the Christian life, or trying to live for themselves on the one hand, and Christ on the other hand. You read the dismal statistics in the first chapter.

Let me deal with one other misunderstanding saturating America and our churches today. Satan has effectively spread this idea so that many have bought into it. The claim is that everybody in America has heard or has the means to hear the Gospel. The Gospel is on radio, TV, and in Christian and other bookstores. Bibles are for sale and available all over, hundreds of thousands of churches fill the land, pastors and evangelists are everywhere spreading the word. We celebrate the birth and resurrection of Christ on major holidays. Therefore, the contention is, no American has an excuse. They could be saved if they wanted to be. That partly absolves us of our responsibility, according to this idea.

Listen, my dear friends. It takes the Holy Spirit to open up the Word of God to us, usually through some concerned witness for Christ. I grew up in a "Christian" home, heard good preaching from the time I was a child, read my Bible, went very faithfully to church, and was baptized at the age of 12. When I went forward and was asked if I believed in Jesus, I said yes, and they told me I was a Christian. I was very sincere and tried to live the Christian life until I was about 24 years old.

I heard many messages on, "Believe on the Lord Jesus Christ and thou shalt be saved." I heard messages on Heaven and Hell. I heard messages on being born-again. During the war, under a savage suicide plane attack, I took out my Bible and saw John 3:16 and John 3:36, and wondered desperately why, since I believed in the Lord Jesus Christ, I did not know for sure if I would go to Heaven or not.

Finally, just before I became a member of a cult, a blessed Baptist pastor in La Grande, Oregon, led me to the Lord Jesus Christ, and I was *saved.*

We are aware that nothing happens, no matter how "expert" we get at witnessing, unless the Holy Spirit works in that person's life.

I have seen the following common mistakes countless times in evangelistic meetings and other outreaches.

People come forward under conviction for their sin. The personal worker, well-meaning and eager, says, "Have you ever asked Christ to come into your heart (life)?" Very often, the person will say, "Yes." Then the personal worker will almost invariably deal with him as a Christian. The lost sinner is puzzled and confused, and likely will not try to be "saved" again.

Chapter Seven – Goodbye Christian America: The Desperate Need of Dying Churches

The questions to ask, when he says he has asked Christ to come into his life, or asked Him to save him, are:

"Did He do it?"

"How do you know?"

"Are you 100 percent sure that if you died right now, you would go to Heaven to be with Jesus?"

Again, "How do you know, and why are you sure?"

We are dealing with the most precious commodity in all the world, an eternal soul that will spend eternity either in Heaven or in Hell. No renowned surgeon has a greater responsibility. Use the Bible. It is by the Holy Spirit acting on the Word of God that brings conviction and salvation to a lost sinner.

Many times, in my own meetings and the meetings of others, such as the great "Word of Life" saint, Jack W., I have double-checked with those who came forward and were supposedly dealt with thoroughly. I discovered, to my consternation and sorrow, that the person believed to be converted did not know whether or not he had been saved, and was confused about the whole transaction. Often, I proceeded then to lead them to Jesus and true salvation.

The advantage of leading them by the Word and the Holy Spirit to a "know-so" salvation is that they are usually thrilled, grateful to Jesus, and eager to follow Him. They also know they did no good works to be saved; Ephesians 2:8-9 is engraved indelibly in their minds. "For by grace are ye saved through faith, and that not of yourselves: it is the gift of God, not of works, lest any man should boast."

In this way, when they are exhorted to do good works in obedience to Jesus, they do not get confused in thinking that it is works that save them, or help save them, but that works demonstrate their love for Jesus, and their salvation.

Many, perhaps thousands, of our "false converts" could be true converts if these simple rules were followed:

1. Get them LOST. They *must* realize that they are lost, one breath from an eternal Hell at any moment. Use the law and the Holiness of God. This allows the Holy Spirit to convict them of their sin and danger.

2. They must know that Jesus is the Eternal God, that He shed His blood for them on the cross, and that He died in their place, was buried, rose bodily from the dead, and now wants to save them forever.

3. They must recognize Jesus as Lord, as well as Savior. Jesus must be accepted for who He is. There is no spiritual dichotomy that allows us to accept a schizophrenic Jesus.

4. They must begin immediately to follow Him and lovingly obey Him. "If any man will come after me, let him deny himself, and take up his cross *daily*, and follow me" (Luke 9:23, emphasis added).

5. They must learn to let Jesus live His life through them, confessing sin, and turning from it the moment they are aware of it.

6. They should begin to share Christ from the very beginning of their Christian life. That way, the joy of Jesus and His

Chapter Seven – Goodbye Christian America: The Desperate Need of Dying Churches

wonderful salvation will be constantly fresh to them, and precious souls can come to Christ.

7. They should begin to study the Word of God, to read it daily, and to tell Jesus every day that they love Him.

8. Follow-up should begin within 24 to 48 hours after the new convert has been saved.

As I related earlier, when I was 12 years old I underwent baptism as a supposed Christian. I was 24 years old when someone finally told me how to be saved and know it. Thank God the suicide planes did not get me, but they got some of my buddies who seemed to be in about the same condition I was in.

One of the sad things I have discovered in hundreds of churches is that when people come forward at the invitation, they are dealt with in front of the whole congregation, with the music still playing, and the people still singing. They are led in a group prayer. That is what happened to me as a 12-year-old boy, and it is still happening in thousands of churches. It is by the marvelous grace of God, and His indefatigable love, that anyone could possibly be saved in such bedlam, but thank God, some are.

How much better it would be, if the inquirers were taken into an inquiry room, carefully questioned, and especially listened to, and their true needs met biblically. Yet the style of invitation is sacred to most churches, so I would at least pray that a thorough follow-up is made, very soon. Ask the convert why they came, what happened, and how they know if they were saved, and/or if their needs were met. This is crucial.

What about the Church? Eighty-eight percent of our youth leave the church at 18. With evolution and atheism, and contempt for the Bible flooding our youth and overwhelming them in college, the news media, and society, the future is bleak indeed, unless God in His sovereign grace breaks in to our society. America, America, the land that I love, the country I volunteered to fight and die for, if necessary, you are so sick, and I weep for you!

Bit by bit, everything the Bible says is right is being declared wrong by today's myopic generation. Spanking: barbaric. The Bible: religious jargon with some truths here and there.

Homosexuals: though condemned in the Bible, really okay, just discriminated against as were the slaves. The absolute fact that they have in their lifetime scores of sexual partners, much horrid disease, STDs, AIDS, a life that is shortened by 30 years or more on average, is of no consequence. That is not even to mention what happens when they meet the God they have spurned, even deluding themselves to believing He approves of their lifestyle.

When a homosexual or a proponent of theirs tells me "they were born that way" (false), I tell them I was born a sinner, but God in His grace saved me, and God will save and change them also, if they confess their sin and come to Him with all their heart.

Chapter Seven – Goodbye Christian America: The Desperate Need of Dying Churches

Then there is abortion, the killing of tens of millions of babies, some by horrific methods, in partial birth abortions. This is a screaming stench in the nostrils of a Holy God, which America, and many of our churches, will be held accountable for.

The first answer? Nationwide repentance and prayer.

If my people, which are called by my name, shall humble themselves, and pray, and seek my face, and turn from their wicked ways; then will I hear from heaven, and will forgive their sin, and will heal their land (II Chronicles 7:14).

Essentially, this is our first, best, and perhaps our only hope. Pastors, Christians in places of power, call for and set up prayer meetings, taking God at His Word. We need national, fervent prayer.

Pastors, evangelists, Bible teachers, I believe in studying through, and preaching and teaching through, the whole Word of God, but this is a major emergency. There will not be another generation to man our churches unless we act now.

Preach on the "gay" life style. Show God's Word and do not be afraid. Do it! Preach on abortion. I did one Sunday, and saw a doctor in my church instantly change and give up abortions. I led him to Christ, along with his wife.

Stand up against the moral turpitude destroying America. Stand up against the pornography shown now even on family TV. Give God's Word on living together without marriage. It is fornication, and condemned, along with those who practice it, by God. Our young people are confused. Love them enough to tell them the truth! Give solid messages on why we attend church.

Show that in any real salvation, faith without works is dead, and cannot save (James 2:14, 2:20).

I am so saddened by the strong, well-known pastors and evangelists, who crumble when pressed on whether or not Jesus is the only way to Heaven. I am ashamed when they hedge their answer, say they do not know, or even suggest Jesus might not be the only way to Heaven.

Yet Jesus clearly said, ". . . I am the way, the truth, and the life; no man cometh unto the Father but by me" (John 14:6). If Jesus is not God, as He claimed, and not the only way to Heaven, to God the Father, then He lied, and Christianity is false, a preposterous and impossible conclusion.

Those who balk at Jesus being the only way to Heaven almost certainly are not true Christians, for that is part of the claim, and part of the package. "Neither is there salvation in any other; for there is none other name under heaven given among men, whereby we must be saved" (Acts 4:12).

Thank God for men like Franklin Graham, who takes no back steps over TV, in the media, or at the White House. When he is told that he cannot pray in the name of Jesus, He declares that He <u>will</u> pray in the name of Jesus, and He <u>does</u>.

Teach our youth, and our adults, about the heroes of the faith, both from Biblical times and now.

Chapter Seven – Goodbye Christian America: The Desperate Need of Dying Churches

From the local pastor and Christians to the megachurches and powerful Christian speakers, we MUST stand unapologetically and boldly for the name of Jesus. Speak the truth in love, but speak up for what the Bible says, no matter what the cost.

Many of our youth are addicted to sex, alcohol, drugs, violence, and immorality in general. They need to hear from God what the consequences are, in this world and the next, and be counseled with kindness, but with prayer and Scripture. They need simultaneously to be bathed in the love of Jesus, and terrified of their offense to a Holy God.

More and more, our families reflect the world's standards. Filth pours from the mouth of our entertainers, and now even from the mouths of many children. Families must be enlisted to reach their children, or they will someday cry over them in Hell. The church must partner with the families to encourage the parents, and help the children and youth.

"Christ Is the Answer" must not be just a slogan, but a fact.

While I would prefer not to be politically involved, we must stand loud and clear against that which destroys America, her values, her youth, and her churches.

It may be that our only recourse now from the incessant revisionists' lies about our history, and Christianity, is to home school our children, however costly that may be. At the very least, we should meet the challenges to the faith of our young people, with excellent films on creation, like Jim Tetlow's super, professionally done, *God of Wonders*. We need

Christians who are scientists to come in and stir up the saints, and answer some of the questions that plague our youth.

We must teach without mincing words about Islamic terrorists, or eventually get squashed by Jihad, or Sharia law, or get our throats slit by those who have sworn to kill all infidels, especially Jews and Christians. Only a few, you say? My sources say that there are millions. Caryl Matriciana has a great teaching film that should be standard for every church, entitled *Islam Rising*. The goal of those terrorists is to conquer the world, and the use of dirty bombs on us is just a matter of time.

Youth rise to challenges. To be entombed in what must seem to them a dead, boring Christianity, will lose them. To follow the blood-red banner of the Lord Jesus Christ into fierce battle to save our churches and once Christian America, to fight not with carnal weapons, but with courage and love and the Spirit of God against impossible odds, will turn many of them back to Jesus, and to the warfare for men's souls. They need a purpose, a burning purpose, and so do we all.

Jesus . . . follow Him!

What we actually need, church-wide and nation-wide, is a mighty revival, if it is not too late in God's timetable for that.

Mark 12:29-31 sums it up so well:

And Jesus answered him, The first of all the commandments is, Hear 0 Israel; The Lord our God is one Lord: And thou shalt love the Lord thy God with all thy heart, and with

Chapter Seven – Goodbye Christian America: The Desperate Need of Dying Churches

all thy soul, and with all thy mind, and with all thy strength: this is the first commandment.

And the second is like, namely this, Thou shalt love thy neighbour as thyself. There is none other commandment greater than these.

Stunningly, God indicates that loving our neighbor is virtually on the same level as loving God, and apparently, any true love for God will be reflected in our love for our neighbor. It would seem to follow logically that if these constitute the greatest commandment, breaking them would be the greatest sin. Though much more is involved than this, we could not help but warn our neighbor if we truly loved the Lord Jesus Christ and He had saved us.

My dear friend, Dr. Mark Williams, who honored me by letting me hold the first evangelistic meetings in his fledgling church in California, may have hit upon the God-given answer to the faltering, failing churches around America, and indeed, around the world. God led Mark as we shared with him personal soul-winning, and God blessed. We saw many saved, with one or more becoming preachers. Mark is now the Executive Vice President of Dynamic Church Planting International.

In a meeting overseas some years ago, around 74 pastors, and churches from about as many nations, invited Dr. Williams to come and teach them how to start churches, particularly daughter churches. (This is where the mother church furnishes some of the people, much prayer, some finances, and oversight to starting a daughter church.) It often increases soul-winning in the new church, and sometimes ignites even the mother church. Dr. Williams, along with Paul Becker and others have set a goal of starting a million churches worldwide through this mother-daughter church-planting concept. In scores of nations worldwide, Mark has trained hundreds of nationals, who have committed themselves to mother-daughter church planting, and training others.

Already, tens of thousands of churches have been started, and something like 2 to 2 ½ million souls have come to Christ! This is one of the most powerful and God-blessed outreaches in the world today. While continuing his worldwide ministry, Dr. Williams is now eyeing America. Please, please get his new book, in which he thoroughly explains how this works, and teaches that virtually any church can do it—start a daughter church. He meets the 12 most common objections, and in winsome joy shares his God-given vision in this new Book, *Winning the World for Christ: The Untapped Potential of Daughter Church Planting.*

Our churches, and America itself, urgently, desperately, need to be baptized in the love of our Lord Jesus Christ, and the subsequent love for each other. Instead, what do our children see? What does the world see? Christians fighting with each other, bickering, murmuring, complaining and being the very hypocrites that we are often charged as being!

It is no wonder our children don't follow in our footsteps; they leave the church in droves. They watch us closely. They watch our lives behind closed doors. They see nothing of the real love of Jesus or love for each other. God commands us in Philippians 2:14-15, "Do everything without complaining or arguing. So that you may become blameless and pure, children of God without fault in a crooked and depraved generation, in which you *shine like stars* in the universe." (Emphasis added) Do we shine like stars?

Our churches are often marked by internal strife and bickering, struggles for control and they have lost sight of a dying world around and *inside* them. Wake up! I Thessalonians 5: 16 "Therefore encourage one another and build each other up. . ." And v. 18, "Be joyful always; pray continually; give thanks in all circumstances, for this is God's will for you in Christ Jesus." Our depraved generation *needs* this.

On the church level, I believe we should study our Bibles systematically, and every six months, give exams to see if we have absorbed the doctrines. We should have lots of fellowship, and fun times, but never let the tail wag the dog.

We should major on teaching how we got our Bible, why we know it is the infallible Word of the one true God. We should thoroughly examine Creation, the attributes of God, the prophecies by the hundreds given and fulfilled in Christ, and soteriology (Biblical doctrine of salvation). We should have missionaries speak, and visit with them often. We should have good studies, and speakers, on apologetics (a rational basis for and defense of the Christian faith).

We should have, and encourage, debates in youth groups, and sometimes publicly, about evolution, origins, legalism, anti-nomianism, the Deity of Christ, the Trinity, etc.

Too often we are looking for a modern day sign, something concrete to hang our faith on, instead of relying on Scripture.

A dear friend, Robert Cedotal, in his Sunday School class, called attention to the response of Jesus to the religious, but mostly lost, scribes and Pharisees, when they asked Him for a sign. "But He answered and said unto them, An evil and an adulterous generation [*America personified today*] seeketh after a sign; and there shall no sign be given to it, but the sign of the prophet Jonas [Jonah]: For as Jonas was three days and three nights in the whale's belly; so shall the Son of man be three days and three nights in the heart of the earth" (Matthew 12:39-40).

Jesus spoke of His bodily Resurrection, the ultimate proof of His Deity, the ultimate confirmation of the Gospel and the power of God. That alone can reach and break the hardened hearts of a perverse generation. Yet how seldom we use it in witnessing and in preaching today. We have relegated it to a much-glamorized Easter Sunday and feel happy to have preserved that. Yet now that the secular society, the ACLU, and the ecumenical disaster of apostate churches insists that all roads lead to God, even that morsel of redemption is being whittled away, bit by bit.

America, our churches, and our people need to hear the resurrection message over and over again, lifting up Jesus, shedding His blood on the cross for us, and climaxing that message constantly with the glorious, powerful, life-changing message of the resurrection of the Lord Jesus Christ! Accord-

Chapter Seven – Goodbye Christian America: The Desperate Need of Dying Churches

ing to God's Word, this is the only hope and the only sign for an evil adulterous generation. Let us, every Christian and preacher of the Gospel, everywhere we go, give that message for America's sake, for the sake of Christianity, and for our sake. With the cross of Jesus, it is the very heart of our message, which is slowly being emasculated. Fire up, step up, pray up, speak up, and watch God work, or consign America and its multitudes to ignominy here, and Hell hereafter!

Most of all, seek by the Word of God and the Holy Spirit to develop a deep love for the Lord Jesus Christ. Continually teach and lead the church, adults, and especially our youth, in soul-winning, sharing testimonies, going out in groups, holding Joy clubs, participating in Bible studies. Celebrate with banquets, prayer meetings of joy, and sometimes brokenhearted repentance.

Years ago, when I was in Seminary, a missionary lady told us, "We must win the battle in the 'heavenlies' against unseen principalities and powers, before we can ever win the war for souls and revival on earth." She was probably quoting from Ephesians 6:12, "For we wrestle not against flesh and blood, but against principalities, against powers, against the rulers of the darkness of this world, against spiritual wickedness in high place." Then we are admonished to take unto us the whole armor of God.

Thank God, Jesus has won the victory over these powerful, deceitful enemies by His death on the cross and subsequent resurrection, but we enter into that victory by faith and believing prayer.

Constantly emphasize that we are in a war to the death with Satan and with the world for the souls of men. Let them know that around the world young people are dying for Jesus Christ. Challenge them; lead them. Again and again take time to look at Jesus, His bloody sacrifice, His love for us, and His command to go to all the world, and preach the Gospel to every creature. Nothing is more thrilling, nothing is more important, nothing has greater rewards.

God help us! The day is far spent. Revive us, O God, and revive our churches. God help our debt-ridden, sex and drug crazed America, and our President, who claims to be a Christian. If he is not, God wake him up, and save him. We care about him, but we are increasingly afraid of him, and his apparent blindness to the mastodonic Muslim threat. He apparently does not know, or does not reveal to the public, that while there are some seemingly friendly verses in the Koran towards people who are not Muslims, there is much severe threatening to those who are not, especially Jews and Christians. The same is true of all non-believers in Islam.

The Caliphs and Muslim authorities have a dreadful weapon. They can declare a Naskh (seemingly contradictory material within or between the twin bases of Islamic holy law) within a Sura (chapter) in the Koran (Qur'an) by inserting a new verse to over-ride the old one. That way, they can have it both ways when they seduce Westerners and others by saying that "the Koran says" when they know very well that verse is as obliterated as if it had never been written. And Muslims *must* honor such changes!

Chapter Seven – Goodbye Christian America: The Desperate Need of Dying Churches

We are in grave and urgent danger inside and outside the church. Call on God now, with all your heart, and share Him, the Lord Jesus Christ, with tears and love, as you have never shared Him before. It may be your last chance. It may be our nation's last chance. We are losing the battle.

When you read the first chapter or two in this book and saw how few really get saved, your eyes may have been opened. It can be very difficult to see through the professing but not possessing Christians cluttering up the church landscape, and lurking in society spreading how disillusioned they are with the church and Christians. From many high schools and colleges, evolution shatters many young believers, contempt for the Bible is epidemic, thousands of cults and false religions, and even some once solid denominations are adding to the confusion.

Real Christians who believe the Bible are held in scorn and contempt, often vilified, and labeled obscurantist bigots, or ignorant hate mongers. History is distorted deliberately to reflect the views of a liberal and unconscionable media and scurrilous "intellectual" revisionists historians, who manage to get their polluted textbooks approved for our schools. The indispensable impact and overwhelming contribution the Bible and Christians made to our Constitution is whittled away, and the Mayflower document declaring that America was being settled to spread the gospel of the Lord Jesus Christ ignored as much as possible.

How on earth can the average American, especially our vulnerable youth, sort it all out, and most wonder why they should even try. Add to that mix, the raging hormones, the old nature, sexually explicit porn, condoms promoted more than Christ, sports, popularity, drugs, sex, and uninformed decisions for Christ, that did not meet their needs or expectations, and you see why I plead with you, dear reader, if you are a true Christian, go reach them for the Lord Jesus Christ with purpose and passion, as Pastor Guy Zerhing did me.

Perhaps we should pay a little closer attention to the story of the Ethiopian eunuch given in Acts, Chapter 8. The eunuch was a man of great authority under Candace, queen of the Ethiopians, having charge of all her treasure. He was an intelligent man, very interested in the portion of the Bible he was reading, the 53rd chapter of Isaiah. He had some contact apparently with believers, and was convicted of his need. He knew about Jesus, but he did not know Jesus as his Lord and Saviour.

Phillip was holding powerful evangelistic meetings with much response in Samaria. To his astonishment, God led him to leave and head for the desert, and join himself to the Ethiopian eunuch and his chariot. Phillip *ran* to the chariot, and saw that the eunuch was reading the prophet Isaiah. (Esaias)

He asked the eunuch a very important and pertinent question. "Understandest thou what thou readest?" The poignant answer was, "How can I except some man should guide me?"

So Phillip opened up the 53rd chapter of Isaiah, which spoke of Jesus and our sin and need, and His sacrifice for us.

Chapter Seven – Goodbye Christian America: The Desperate Need of Dying Churches

Acts 8:35, "Then Phillip opened his mouth and began at the same scripture and preached unto him Jesus."

The eunuch believed, as Phillip admonished him, "with all thine heart," and subsequently as a new believer, declaring that he believed that "Jesus Christ is the Son of God," went down into a certain water and was baptized.

He had the Bible, he wanted to know the truth, yet he did not understand, until a Spirit-filled man opened up the Scriptures to him. So many today, even many professing Christians are crying out, "How can I understand, except some man should show me?"

How tragic, and how pitiful!

I was a missionary to Alaska, and still would be except for age and a heart transplant. I have wept and prayed for a lost world, for men and women who have never heard of our Lord Jesus Christ. Hundreds of millions of them.

Yet we do not realize that America is increasingly a mission field as well. Please dear fellow Christians, millions are unsaved right here in America, in society, and in our churches. Let us go in the love of Jesus, help them to understand, and point them to the Lord Jesus Christ!

> Please help. If you feel this book will help jar your group or church, would you suggest it or buy it for them? Or maybe ask that your Church Leaders use it for Soul-Winning Classes? Start a class of your own. Use it for Bible study classes. People are lost and God wants us to share the Cross, share Jesus. Will you help us? Buy ten copies and share. Contact the publisher and we will be glad to sell books for these causes at deep discounts.

National Prayer

"A Prayer of Repentance"

This prayer has been attributed to Evangelist Billy Graham and to the late Paul Harvey of radio fame, ("The Rest of the Story") however Billy Graham did not use it and I rather doubt Paul Harvey did either.

The original version was written by Pastor Bob Russell and offered at a Governor's prayer breakfast in Frankfort, Kentucky, in 1995. It came to national prominence when it was revised by Rev. Joe Wright, Senior Pastor of the Central Christian Church in Wichita, and offered during an opening session, at the Kansas House of Representatives, in 1996. It caused quite a stir.

Afterwards, Rev. Joe Wright was quoted as saying, "I certainly did not mean to be offensive to individuals, but I don't apologize for the truth." He also said, "The problem I guess, is that you're not supposed to get too specific when you talk about sin."

The prayer was read a month later by the Chaplain coordinator in the Nebraska legislature and again created a firestorm. It was reportedly read in the Colorado legislature later that year.

This should be America's National Prayer and it is easy to see why God has used it. It is certainly relevant today.

National Prayer

We come before You today to ask Your Forgiveness and seek Your direction and guidance. We know Your Word says, "Woe to those who call evil good," but that's exactly what we have done. We have lost our Spiritual equilibrium and inverted our values.

- *We confess that; we have ridiculed the absolute truth of Your Word and called it pluralism;*
- *We have worshipped other gods and called it multiculturalism;*
- *We have endorsed perversion and called it an alternative lifestyle;*
- *We have exploited the poor and called it the lottery;*
- *We have neglected the needy and called it self-preservation;*
- *We have rewarded laziness and called it welfare;*
- *We have killed our unborn and called it choice;*
- *We have shot abortionists and called it justifiable;*
- *We have neglected to discipline our children and called it building self-esteem;*

- *We have abused power and called it political savvy;*
- *We have coveted our neighbor's possessions and called it ambition;*
- *We have polluted the air with profanity and pornography and called it freedom of expression;*
- *We have ridiculed the time-honored values of our forefathers and called it enlightenment.*

Search us, O God, and know our hearts today; try us and see if there be some wicked way in us; cleanse us from every sin and set us free. Guide and bless these men and women who have been sent here by the people of this state and who have been ordained by You, to govern this great state of Kansas. Grant them your wisdom to rule and may their decisions direct us to the center of Your Will.

I ask in the name of your Son, The Living Savior, Jesus Christ.

Instead of the great state of Kansas, we need to apply this to the Late Great America and to the Late Great American Church!

Other Books by Floyd C. McElveen

McElveen has over 1.1 million books in print, with 360,000 copies in Russia of *Evidence You Never Knew Existed* that is also published in Russia as *The Compelling Christ*, but most often under the title of *Facts You Need to Know About*.

This book is published by the thousands in China in Simplified Chinese and Mandarin, and in Korea. It has also been translated and published in Romania. Pastors are using the English version for outreach and discipleship, ordering and distributing hundreds of copies of this small but powerful book in their communities and to their people for outreach.

With the Bible League projects now complete, McElveen's books are in eight or nine languages. He recently wrote a book, published by Huntington Press, *The Disney Boycott*. It is clear, concise, and gets to the heart of the real issue regarding the homosexual lifestyle being promoted by Disney.

McElveen's latest book, published by Big Mac Publishers, is perhaps the crowning jewel, *So Send I You* (previously as *Unashamed, A Burning Passion to Share Christ*), which was endorsed by Dr. John Ankerberg, Dr. John Morris, the late Jerry Falwell, and others.

Other books McElveen has written include, *The Beautiful Side Of Death*, *The Mormon Illusion*, currently published by Kregel, and *God's Word, Final, Infallible and Forever*, published by Gospel Truth Ministries, *Faith of an Atheist*, published by Big Mac Publishers, and *The Call of Alaska*, published by Promise Publishers. This book was subsidy-published, financed by Rocky McElveen, one of McElveen's sons.

For those interested in *Evidence You Never Knew Existed*, the book can be ordered individually or in bulk from Gospel Truth Ministries,

Fax 616-451-8907, or Ph. 616-451-4562, or Gospel Truth Ministries, 1340 Monroe Avenue, N.W., Grand Rapids, Michigan 49505.

Recently, McElveen has written a book, and acted as producer of *Jesus Christ-Joseph Smith, a Search for the Truth*, in a DVD, with over 500,000 copies now distributed in English and thousands more translated into Spanish. The DVD is based on the book of the same title.

Any effort not glorifying God is futile, but we pray and believe God has led us in this effort to shock the Christian Church in America.

Pastor/Missionary Floyd McElveen
and his beautiful wife, Virginia.

If this book has been a blessing to you, encouraged you, or helped motivate you to be a soul-winner, please share with us. If you have questions, please contact Mac or Virginia McElveen, by email: mac4christ@comcast.net or snail mail: 16 Sweet Bay Trail, Petal, MS 39465, or phone: 1-601-584-7123.

Printed in the United States
221634BV00002B/1/P